Joy Comes with the Mourning

A STUDY OF LOSS, GRIEF, & RUNAWAY PIGS

Janis Shanahan Miller

ISBN 979-8-35093-357-4 eBook 979-8-35093-358-1

Parish Design Company
Patrick S. Miller
Minden, LA
patrick@parishdesignco.com

THIS BOOK IS WRITTEN to bring hope and comfort to those who have suffered with losses in their lives, reminding them of the glories of God, the promises of Christ and the abiding presence of the Holy Spirit.

Written in memory of Captain Max Robert "Cappy" Miller, beloved husband and friend for fifty-three years, and dedicated to my two sons, Patrick and Ryan, who have provided so many of the memorable and joyful moments in my life, to my grandchildren, Lela Margaret, Treat, Shirley Cate, Gracie, and Max, who are helping me to make my new memories, and to College Hill Presbyterian Church, Oxford, Mississippi—they were and are the ultimate grief counselors.

AUTHOR'S NOTE

This book is filled with stories about my life and my family because that is the subject matter about which I know the most. However, the stories are only the introductions to the greater story: the gospel of Jesus Christ. Each chapter concludes with a "truth of God" I learned as I dealt with loss and grief. The study questions at the end of each chapter are questions I asked myself on my journey to emotional recovery. I hope you, the reader, will laugh at the stories and allow them to lift your heart so that, for a moment, your frame of mind will be buoyed, bringing you a more hopeful perspective from which you can see the immense importance of Christ's healing love and sacrifice as it relates to your life.

Janis Shanahan Miller

CONTENTS

INTRODUCTION

Nehemiah in Legoland

"For the good hand of my God was upon me."

Nehemiah 2:8

At last, the "Grands" had headed home after doing an adequate job of picking up the scattered Lego pieces. As children love to do, they had each built Lego forts, using some of the long but not quite forgotten larger Duplo blocks from their toddler years—Duplo blocks made much better fortifications. They then proceeded to wage war on each other's forts, crafting Lego catapults and rocket launchers that hurled paper wads. The violence escalated to launching miniature marshmallows, though that portion of the siege had to be suspended due to the marshmallow-eating cat who changed his allegiance to the combatants depending on which side had the most "ammunition" stockpiled.

Finally, the battle became serious. Duplo blocks left over from building the walls of the forts sailed through the air, striking furniture, their grandmother, and, occasionally, the enemy's walls. The two sides eventually met for peace accords, sharing their K-rations of cookies and hot chocolate topped with whipped cream since all the marshmallows had been used for projectiles.

Following the signing of the treaty, the mop-up of the battlefield ensued with most of the Legos and Duplos put in their appropriate places, to be used for the next global onslaught. I say "most" because some Legos are always missed—Legos the cat mistakes for marshmallows and deposits in his food bowl for further snacking, Legos that drop down the heater vents and aren't found until the next winter when the smell of melted plastic wafts through the house, or the lone Lego that someone dropped on the way to the bathroom, which I step on in the middle of the night.

It was this last sleep-depriving Lego that put me in mind of the walls the children had built to protect their respective kingdoms or, more correctly, the rebuilding of those walls after an enemy attack. Rebuilding is what one does after having suffered a loss. That loss may be a job that ended, the death of a friend, or spouse or the loss felt through a destructive relationship. It may be the loss of the ability to do an activity you once enjoyed but can no longer do. It may be a divorce or having to move to a new, strange place. And as a country, it may be the collective sense of loss when we endure a "9/11" or cope with a virus that completely changes how we live. In whatever way loss is encountered, it breaks down the walls of the safe, sane existence we have always lived, and those walls are not made out of Legos. Rather, they are made out of ideals, emotions, relationships, companionship, communication, and, if you're a Christian, faith.

My walls began to crumble when my husband was killed in a horrific car accident. I got called to the scene, believing it had been a "fender bender" and that my husband, Max Robert, needed a ride home. Without an ounce of fear or dread, I drove alone to the site of the accident. My mind could barely cope with the carnage I saw when I arrived at the scene, with an almost unrecognizable truck at the bottom of a gully and the Life Flight helicopter transporting the young man who had hit Max to the nearest trauma center.

My walls continued to break down when I was asked to drive to a small country hospital where they had taken my husband; I was given no information, no warning, as to his condition. My fortifications—emotion, companionship, communication, and ideals—had taken a direct hit, and the only remaining support that held up the last vestige of my walls was my faith, and I began to sing.

I sang "It Is Well with My Soul" as I drove to that country hospital, remembering the times I had tried to envision this moment that we all dread but which we all must face. Would I be strong? Would my faith continue to support me? Would I be angry with God if, as I feared, Max was dead?

When I reached the hospital, I sat silently in my car and reflected on the song I had been singing during the thirty-minute drive. It was *not* well with my soul, but I *wanted* it to be, and that desire was enough to see me through many dark days.

The book of Nehemiah describes the author as being faced with dark days as he too tried to rebuild a wall–the wall surrounding the city of Jerusalem. He encountered disbelief among the people of Jerusalem, who said that it could not be done. Still, he exhorted them mightily to join in the rebuilding. He was up against an ever-approaching deadline to complete the wall, and he had to use part of his Hebrew workforce to guard against the enemies who would seek to destroy the work before it could be completed. So, what did Nehemiah do? He **prayed** to the one true God that He would be in the midst of the rebuilding.

Rebuilding life after loss looks a little like Nehemiah's efforts. Are we where we are supposed to be in the grieving process amidst the rubble of our loss? Are we beginning to exhibit disbelief that God is even there? Do people do and say things that unintentionally cause us more pain? Are we given tools, some by the way of books that, rather than lifting us up, actually bring us further down? Do we attend grief recovery programs where the outcome is more shared sorrow and no sense of recovery? Surely, in the midst of grief, God wants us to try to focus on Him and the joy He has provided in our lives rather than the losses brought about by a broken world.

I wrote *Joy Comes with the Mourning* to let you know that I understand about standing in the rubble of a life broken by grief and to remind you of God's gift of joy even as we suffer sorrow. And I wrote this book as an alternative to other books on loss—books that only seem to deepen your sense of loss rather than lift your spirits.

I know the pain of having your walls destroyed. Mine were smashed, leaving me without mortar, trowels, and most of my familiar building blocks. But the one lone building block waiting to be placed in just the right spot, was faith. This book is built on that one block and is comprised of unique anecdotes of my hilarious, chaotic life as I attempted to rebuild my walls. It is filled with the truths that God taught me, which became the mortar, the trowel, and the blocks of brick for my walls, with Christ being my cornerstone. It is meant to make you smile or laugh out loud, if only for a moment, and to reflect on how your rebuilding is going.

Nehemiah didn't just build a wall; he also built gates that allowed traffic to flow in and out of the city. As we rebuild after loss, it is important to include gates as well, so that relationships, ideals, emotions, communications, and faith can once again come into your life to support you and bring a measure of joy to your day-to-day living. Please allow this book to come through the gates of your walls, filling you with God's words while reading about dead horses, runaway pigs, and roller-skating librarians. As you read, I hope the words of the stories and the words of the Holy Scriptures will fill you with joy that comes not from mourning a loss but from the morning light as it reflects the love of our Savior, Jesus Christ. And like Nehemiah, pray.

If this book was about the very popular movie, *The Lego Movie*, I would be singing its award-winning theme song, "Everything Is Awesome," but I think I'll stick with "It Is Well with My Soul" because it finally is.

CHAPTER 1

Cats on a Plane

Inspired by the movie *Snakes on a Plane*

---

*"But thanks be to God who in Christ always leads us
in triumphal procession, and through us spreads the
fragrance of the knowledge of him everywhere."*

2 Corinthians 2:14

My young grandson, Max, had just helped me carry in the last of
the groceries and we began putting them away. He was trying to earn some
money so he could buy a bow and arrow set once he convinced his parents
that he would not use it in the house or against his sisters. Putting the groceries away was the last of the agreed-upon chores and I went to pay him,
at which point I realized I'd lost my wallet.

Panic immediately set in as I imagined all the terrible implications of
losing my credit cards, insurance cards, drivers' license, and so on. Being
an exceedingly logical six-year-old, Max suggested I look in my purse, with
his sound thinking revealing that I had lost my purse, my cell phone and
car keys as well. Max, besides having a logical mind also has wicked sense
of humor and suggested that perhaps I'd lost all my marbles as well.

Ignoring the six-year-old comedian, I back-tracked my movements from the time we returned from the market and realized I'd left my purse in the car when we got home. I rushed to the garage and thankfully retrieved my purse, phone, and car keys. Neither the wallet nor the marbles were yet to be found.

Max and I searched high and low in the car, pantry shelves, kitchen drawers, coat pockets, and discarded grocery bags. It was only when I took time out from the search to fix Max some lunch, which included a glass of chocolate milk, that the wallet turned up, tucked safely away in the refrigerator in the bag that contained the milk. But my marbles were still lost... and then I lost my husband.

I miss my husband! Everyone called him "Captain" for his rank, having served twenty-five years in the US Coast Guard; I called him by his middle name, Bob, throughout our high school days and changed to calling him by his given name, Max, after he entered the service of our country. The grandchildren called him "Cappy." And to say I miss him encompasses so many feelings–faith in the sovereignty of God, my sorrow at the loss of my love and best friend, frustration at being left alone to deal with the difficulties of life, longing for his presence, and joy for all the years and memories we shared. I smile when I look at his picture, thinking about the simple things I miss most.

I miss holding hands as we walked through the parking lot at the grocery store. I miss his fussing at the cat, knowing he'd always relent and let her snuggle next to him each night. I miss the Captain's cooking, especially since we both knew I couldn't cook. Case in point: he took my first attempt at meatloaf and offered it to a stray dog who, just as he had done, declined to eat it.

I miss antiquing with him, though my search to find that perfect piece of furniture for our home often ended in his finding the perfect Budweiser beer mug to add to his collection. I miss his pacing during tight football games and eating homemade chili with him on cold evenings. I miss traveling in the car with the Captain when we would harmonize with the songs on the radio, knowing he would make up words when he couldn't remember the lyrics. He sang his version with such gusto and assurance that I frequently came to believe that the lyricist got it wrong: "You and me, endlessly" became "you and me and Leslie." I often wondered who Leslie was.

But what I miss most about my husband are his hugs. Max gave great hugs; his big arms wrapped around me and held me tight, keeping me safe in his embrace. And as he held me, I breathed in the scent of his aftershave. In high school, it was British Sterling or English Leather, but as we grew older, he gravitated toward Calvin Klein's Obsession. I've kept the Captain's last bottle, sometimes spraying it on one of his shirts I wear while painting. Just last week, the scent of his aftershave flooded my mind with a memory, and I chuckled, thinking about a long-forgotten time when we took the family cat on a plane ride from Alaska to Texas.

We were in the last four seats of an Alaskan Airlines "red-eye" as it flew through the night from Anchorage, Alaska, to Houston, Texas. Max and I sat side-by-side with our two sons across the aisle from us and the family cat in a carrier lodged under the seat in front of me. Unlike today, when people travel with their therapy cats, therapy dogs, therapy peacocks, therapy snakes, and other "necessary" creatures, Pywackett was just our family pet and, as such, had to be contained in an ASPCA-approved cat carrier. Unfortunately, the ASPCA did not consider the litter box needs of a cat on a nine-hour flight or the reaction of said cat when the plane encountered a thunderstorm. With the first big bump and clap of thunder, Pywackett let out a howl that raised the collective blood pressure of passengers and crew. Aromatically speaking, Pywackett also let something else out, and though I tried to pretend the sudden stench was a bag of rancid peanuts, the nearby passengers awoke to an odor reminiscent of a skunk that had eaten broccoli.

Our two sons, both former Boy Scouts like their father, quickly realized the peanut story was "fake news" and jumped into action. One retrieved Max's shaving kit from under the seat and snatched the bottle of Calvin Klein's Obsession, while the other grabbed the ASCPA-approved cat carrier and fled to the bathroom adjacent to our seats. How both of our six-foot-plus sons along with a cat carrier managed to get into a single airplane bathroom, I will never know. I do know that when the door to that bathroom opened, the feline stench was gone, replaced by the overpowering allure of Obsession. And while I am sure the boys meant to give the cat a quick spritz, evidently there had been a sibling struggle over who would do the spritzing. About half a bottle of aftershave was doused on the cat.

Suddenly, other passengers began to complain about sinus headaches and fragrance allergies. Our family of four sat straight-faced with innocent expressions and prayed for a tailwind to get us to our destination more quickly.

Upon arriving at the Houston airport, we realized the hotel shuttle probably would not want our odiferous family on board, so I headed for the ladies' room (the cat was a female too) and tried to wash her in the sink. The washing part was met with growls and whines, but there was no outright feline insurrection until I foolishly headed to the hand dryer. I do recall the kindness my husband showed me at the first aid station, where he tried to explain away my clothes infused with both cat hair and aftershave while the smirking attendant apologized for having to use so many tiny Hello Kitty adhesive bandages on my arms. She claimed she was only used to dealing with small children, not big babies.

The trip my husband and I took for so many years of life cannot be compared with a plane ride, a cruise ship, or even a visit to the grocery store. My flesh-and-blood traveling companion is gone, but because of Christ's covenant with us both, my memory of the Captain travels with me, and the uplifting support I feel from that memory, along with the help of the Holy Spirit, is enough to sustain me.

I've heard it said that powerful memories are most often evoked by our sense of smell. Indeed, Proverbs 27:9 says, "Oil and fragrance make the heart glad." And Paul shares the importance of fragrance in Ephesians 5:1–2: "Therefore be imitators of God as beloved children; And walk in love as Christ loved us and gave himself for us, a fragrant offering and sacrifice to God." The "fragrant offering" of Max's aftershave was the catalyst that evoked my memories and brought me closer to some truths that God intended for me to learn.

Remembering our losses in life is a natural occurrence that can immobilize us with grief. As I wrestled with my painful memories of a crushed truck and a husband lying dead, I knew I needed a means to counterbalance those memories. I specifically set out thinking about and doing other things. After starting and ending each day with a prayer of thanksgiving to God, my solace was found in music—playing the piano, listening to music, rereading the words to favorite hymns. In the evening, which was the most difficult time for me, I would lose myself in a good mystery. The point is that I did not allow myself to live in a constant state of grief.

Finding a momentary alternative to grief is paramount to becoming emotionally healthy. For the reader, it may be as simple as taking a walk, reading a book, painting a picture, writing a song, or trying a new recipe so that the mind has a chance to recharge before you face your grief again. Misery needs to be given a short rest.

Praying a prayer of thanksgiving each day may seem counter to the loss you are trying to overcome, but "misery loves company," and when we pray, we are in the company of the Lord, who understands our loss because of the death of His Son on the cross. And knowing that God understands our grief can help lift the heavy burden of painful memories.

As painful as any loss may be, the memories of that loss can actually be an experience of personal growth. It can be a time of sharing your feelings by talking to a good friend, starting a journal of your thoughts, pouring out your sorrows to the Lord, or just sitting quietly and contemplating the events that have shaped your life. In sharing or reliving those memories, one can begin to see an honest, whole image of your life—past, present and future—and how God figures into that life.

The very act of remembering is an instrumental element in the Holy Scriptures. The following three references illustrate the importance of memory, and may bring the reader a better understanding of how remembrance is a good and godly thing.

Most will remember the story of Noah, the ark, and the great flood, where God destroyed the people of the earth who had been corrupted by evil. When the flood waters subsided, God made a promise to mankind that He would never flood the earth again. He set the first rainbow in the sky as a reminder of that promise. Today, the image of the rainbow has been drawn into political turmoil, but for God's people, it is a symbol of God's truthfulness and promise to fulfill His covenant with them: "I will remember my covenant that is between me and you and every living creature of all flesh" (Genesis 9:15). Memory, in this case, serves to highlight God's promise and His special relationship with mankind.

Jesus, himself, illustrated the importance of "remembering" when He established Holy Communion with the breaking of the bread and the drinking of the wine, forever symbolizing the body and blood of Christ: "Do this in remembrance of me" (Luke 22:19b). And while this verse is one most of us have committed to memory, it is the previous portion of that verse that should come to mind with equal importance: "And when He had given thanks, He broke it" (Luke 22:19a). Not only were the disciples asked to remember the breaking of the bread and the drinking of the wine, but it was made clear that giving thanks was to be part of that memory. Christ knew He was to be betrayed. Christ knew He was to be unfairly tried. Christ knew He was to suffer a horrible death but still He remembered to give thanks. Memories can remind us to give thanks, even in the midst of tragedy.

A final example of the importance of memories in the Bible comes from the words of a convicted thief hanging on a cross: "Jesus, remember me when you come into your kingdom. And He said to him, 'Truly, I say to you, today you will be with me in paradise'" (Luke 23:42–43). Two men, both condemned—one guilty and one innocent—shared a memory that would last an eternity.

Good memories can bring one continuous joy, but it is understood that not all memories are good. Memories of loss, sadness, betrayal, and desperation can continue to cause feelings of sorrow, anger and fear. But when memories are seen through the lens of God's sovereignty, they provide spiritual growth and peace, knowing that God is in control.

The Scriptures show us that memory can lead us to rest in God's promises of mercy, can help us to give thanks in the midst of tragedy and, like a condemned man two thousand years ago, memory can offer hope.

Know that God in Christ remembers your grief with His unfailing, unearned love while leading us to the acceptance of memories, good and bad, and this directs us to peace in our hearts and minds.

Therefore, let us revel in those aromas, those fragrances, those memories that remind us of the "fragrant offering" of Christ and bring all our senses into a complete awareness of what He has done for you, for me, and for Captain Max.

Reflections:

1. What is the earliest memory you have, and how does it make you feel?

2. Is there one thing that evokes memories more than any other thing in your life?

3. Is the gospel of Christ a factor when you remember happy things? Unhappy things? Read Psalm 105:4–5, 8.

4. How do your memories help to establish a Christian living pattern for today? Read Psalm 143:10–12.

"The memory of the righteous is a blessing."

Proverbs 10:7a

CHAPTER 2

"There's No Place Like Home"

Dorothy Gale from *The Wizard of Oz*

"For we know that if the tent that is our earthly home
is destroyed, we have a building from God."

2 Corinthians 5:1

After my husband died so suddenly, everyone advised me not to make any major decisions until one year had passed. What most of those well-meaning friends did not understand was that just getting up each morning and deciding to make it through the day was a major decision. Being seen at the grocery store after losing the Captain was a major decision. Singing a special hymn in church that was a favorite for us both was a major decision. But I suppose most people meant that a decision such as moving to a new place would qualify as "major." And thus, I did consider such a move, and like the impulsive person I am, I followed through with that decision before the first year was up.

The desire to run away from our home was strong, in part because Max wasn't there anymore and yet, I "saw" him everywhere. Coupled with the intimidation I felt when facing the John Deere tractor, the copperhead snake in my art room, the red wasps on my front porch or the unpaid mortgage, and even most people could understand my desire to "flee."

The live copperhead in my art room almost did it for me. I hate snakes—if only Eve had had such an aversion—and what I hate even more is dismembering snakes. After saving the cat from the peril she faced in her attempt to use the copperhead as a plaything, I ran through my usual bouts of hysteria, gnashing my teeth, and wishing the Captain was there to save me before I hitched up my pants (pajama bottoms) and got out the shovel. Because my aversion to snakes is closely followed by an aversion to blood and guts, I closed my eyes as I brought the shovel down and succeeded only in cutting off the tip of the serpent's tail, a misaimed act that not only failed to kill the snake but made it extremely cranky. I called my son and let him finish the job.

That night, my son and I talked about how hard it was for me to be in this house by myself, and I ruminated on where I would move if I decided that moving was my best course of action. He reminded me that his dad's first criteria for a good place to live was the presence and quality of the local donut shop. But with nineteen moves under my belt, I was an expert on more than just donuts. Still, the question lingered as to where I could go that would make me feel better. I began to reminisce about our former places of residence, along with the pros and cons associated with each one: the cost of housing, the cost of food, the cost of utilities, the percentage of sales tax, the price of gasoline, and the presence of snakes.

As for the price of gasoline, I could not beat our time in Alaska, nor could I discount the sheer magnificence of the place. And while I'm sure snakes are in Alaska, I never saw one. However, the threat of moose and bears ran a close second to the snakes, bears in particular. Statistics show that more people are killed every year by moose attacks than by bears; they were not the picture of Rocky and Bullwinkle from my youth. But the image of large claws and sharp teeth tearing me limb from limb made a greater impression than antlers.

I remembered that old Alaskan adage regarding claws and teeth: "Brown, lie down; black, run back." I think I first saw these instructions tied to the "bear bells" for sale in several tourist shops. These bells were attached to hiking sticks that were for sale and touted as the necessary equipment for a walk on the wild side of the "Last Frontier." The bells, not the sticks, were advertised as being the first line of defense against the ravenous local predators, and it was the tinkling of the little brass bells that was purported to strike terror in any nearby bear. I remember my husband likening the "bear bells" to a dinner bell, and that is perhaps why the bell/stick manufacturers attached their second line of defense in the form of that nifty little poem. The problem with the poem was twofold: first, you had to get close enough to said bear to identify its type/color, and second, you had to decide your course of action *very quickly!*

The poem's interpretation was that if you encounter a brown bear named Grizzly, you should lie down and play dead since grizzly bears like to play with their food before they eat it, much like our two sons did with their meals. But I never saw our sons turn down a meal simply because it wasn't fun. Nor did I believe the dead act would fool a grizzly bear. The dinner bell had rung!

As for the "black, run back" part of the instructions, this referenced the Alaskan black bear, which, though not as large as a grizzly, didn't care if its prey was animated or not. He just wanted to eat you, thus exposing the fallacy of the second set of instructions in the poem. "Running back" from a black bear had an extremely low rate of success. Indeed, one enterprising Anchorage gentleman used a black bear as a murder weapon by trailing raw meat throughout his house, with those meaty snacks leading to his wife. The black bear did not go to jail, but his accomplice did.

Together, Max and I decided that should we encounter either type of bear, our only hope was that we could get him to choke on the bear bells before he choked on us. And with that, I decided that Alaska was out!

Crossing Alaska off my list along with Virginia/Washington D.C. (too many politics), Maryland (love the Orioles, hate crab cakes), New Orleans (love the Saints, hate crawfish étouffée) or Texas (love the Astros, hate the snakes and tarantulas), that left our home state of California.

Growing up in Bakersfield, California, was a wondrous time, full of summer snipe hunts in the field behind my house, going with Max to the drive-in movie or Stans Burger Drive-In, deftly performing Chinese fire drills on Chester Ave, pretending we didn't hear our parents calling us to come home from a game of flashlight tag, and drinking out of the garden hose when we got thirsty. We rode our bikes without helmets, went waterskiing at Lake Ming, and said prayers at football games. Christmas vacation was called Christmas vacation, not winter holidays, and Easter vacation was always the week before Easter Sunday; there were no spring breaks or trips to Florida beaches. We collected canned food for distribution at Thanksgiving, and we always put money in the red kettle of the Salvation Army at Christmas. We knew never to step on the black-topped road at the height of summer because our flip-flops would stick to the scorching asphalt. It was a time when children still set up neighborhood lemonade stands, with the lemonade being made using the water from the aforementioned garden hose. We truly lived in a magical kingdom, suntanned, healthy, and full of hope.

That magical kingdom has ceased to be magical, and if I were to move back to California, I could choose either to buy a house or to buy food, but considering the cost of real estate, I couldn't do both. And if I decided that housing trumped eating, I'd have to consider the perils of home ownership in the Golden State as it is today.

I toured some of the neighborhoods there and was dismayed at my findings. Many of the houses had no yards because of the terrible drought California had been suffering, and the lawns had just been paved and painted green. Sadly, this did away with the requirement of a garden hose, one of my favorite sources of drinking water. I noticed a sign at an elementary school close to the neighborhood I was touring where its marquee gave the dates for its "winter holidays"; this seemed a contradiction in terms for an area covered with palm trees and billboards for Coppertone Suntan Oil and Jamaica Joe sunglasses.

The neighborhood also sported what were considered "starter" homes, whose prices started at $500,000. They came with three fireplaces and three-car garages. I guess the three fireplaces were because of those "winter" holidays, and I surmised that the third bay of the garages must house the snowplows for the same reason.

The final decision was made when I attempted to drive on the Southern California freeway system, roads on which I had learned to drive, but which had since become gridlocked parking lots in times of high traffic and racecourses during slack hours.

As I pondered the uniqueness of each of our duty stations, I realized that the best place I could live was right where I was, in the house Max and I had chosen together in the small town of Oxford, Mississippi. Here, I pass by lemonade stands on street corners, stopping to buy a cup, knowing the garden hose is nearby. Fireflies flitter and blink in the summer nights, with children ignoring the calls of their parents while they try to catch just one more "light" and there are the snipe hunts along the levee where nothing is ever caught but the tales of the "one that got away" become the stuff of legends at the dinner table.

And then there is my family: my two sons, their wives and the "Grands." Little Gracie came into the bathroom one day as I was pulling up the top of my swimsuit. In a shocked voice, she pointed to my chest and asked, "What are those?" I gently answered that those were my bosoms and that her mother had some just like them (her mother is a size four petite). Gracie, with her hand on her three-year-old hip, declared, "Oh no, she doesn't." Could I get that honesty anywhere else?

Little Max came over from next door one evening for a post-bath surprise visit—a surprise for both me and his parents, who thought he was safely tucked in his bed. Ever the Captain's quick-witted namesake, he realized that it had started to rain and that his feet would get muddied when returning from his visit, thus giving irrefutable proof that he had left the house after his bath. From behind a door, I watched him put a pair of my oven mitts on his feet and walk home, leaving his parents to wonder how low my cooking skills had sunk because of my muddy oven mitts left at their doorstep.

I awoke one morning to loud hammering and looked out the window to see Shirley Cate nailing boards to the oak tree just outside my bedroom window. The next thing I knew, she had built the perfect tree fort out of her Cappy's scrap wood, hoisted his old pirate flag, and completed her project with a dumbwaiter of sorts so she could pull up the snacks she had pilfered from my kitchen snack drawer.

Lela Margaret still loves to make Cappy's recipe for "dough biscuits" and never fails to write me the sweetest letters when she's been here for a visit. And Treat lets me throw the football with him, build Legos with him, and watch *The Avengers* movies with him. Three-car garages could not bring me this kind of joy.

Finally, my husband's words of wisdom came back to me in the form of a fragrant aroma that titillated my taste buds and filled my mind with loving thoughts of him. He always said that a town was only as good as its donut shop. And there it is, right off the town square. I walk in and spot them–the buttermilk old-fashioneds. While they are not my favorites, they were Max's, so I buy some, though I can't abide the strong "wheelhouse" coffee he would have added to his order. Billy Graham once said that heaven is the most perfect place any of us can imagine. Believing that to be true, I suspect that in the Captain's new home, he's eating donuts that are utterly divine and sipping "wheelhouse" coffee that is simply heavenly.

Donuts notwithstanding, it is obvious that deciding on the place to call home seemed monumental after Max died. Making *any* decision is monumental after any kind of loss. However, I found great comfort in

Proverbs 16:33 that says, "The lot is cast into the lap but every decision is from the LORD." Another scripture that impacted my decision-making was Paul's letter to the Ephesians: "Try to discern what is pleasing to the Lord" (Ephesians 5:10). So, I rested in the wisdom of the Lord, watching and listening for His guidance and affirmation. This meant praying and studying His Word. With my focus shifted to pleasing the Lord, I was no longer casting about, seeking the advice of others, with decisions seeming more like whims than prudent, decisive actions. And from that study, I came to know a peace that helped me to slow down, consider my path forward, and truly see what God had provided for me in my current situation.

Where I live now seems to please God, the location of which is of little consequence because of my ultimate home with Him. And yet, God has seen fit to surround me with not just my family but His family in the form of my church and my community. In a time of loss, we all need the love and support of others, and if you are not blessed as I am to have your family close by, then I pray you will choose to have God's family of believers at your side. C.S. Lewis, in his book, *Mere Christianity,* explains the need for God's family this way: "That is why the Church, the whole body of Christians showing Him to one another is so important. You might say when two Christians are following Christ together there is not twice as much Christianity as when they are apart but sixteen times as much. Consequently, the one really adequate instrument for learning about God is the whole Christian community, waiting for Him together."[3] This family will exhort you, support you, and remind you that this home we have here is but for a moment until we move into our new home with the Lord, in a shining new Jerusalem. When we are surrounded by the body of Christ, we are protected by His wall of love and forgiveness, and we are adopted into His family. We will pray with greater intent, sing with greater joy, proclaim the name of Jesus even louder, and give thanks to a loving God who has declared that there will be a welcome mat for us, leading to the home that has been prepared ahead of time by our Creator, our Savior, and our Sustainer.

Reflections

1. What comes to mind when you think about the word "home?"

2. What do you think it means "to feel at home?"

3. Name three places that have made you "feel at home" and ask yourself why you felt that way. Was one of them church? If so, why? If not, why not?

4. How do you picture your final home with God?
   Read Revelation 21:1–4, 10–11.

"Jesus answered him, 'If anyone loves me, he will keep my word, and my Father will love him and we will come to him and make our home with him.'"

John 14:23

CHAPTER 3

Howdy Doody in Full Metal Jacket

"For the LORD sees not as a man sees; man looks on the
outward appearance, but the LORD looks on the heart."

1 Samuel 16:7b

I'm sitting at my desk, looking out on the lake and the backyard. The firepit is stacked with wood, ready for the next marshmallow roast, though it's raining today. Rebuilding it with dry wood tomorrow will give me something to do. I'm at loose ends right now as I'm out of a job. My previous one ended when I was robbed at work, and I realized that the cost of going through all that fear and chaos again was not worth it. I could be cleaning the house for an activity, and I'm probably the only person I know who has four vacuum cleaners. My excuse today is that vacuuming scares the cat. I could make some meals ahead to avoid cooking dinner each night, but you know how I am with cooking. I could paint a picture, but the art room is clean and snake-free which leaves me with only two options: junk food therapy and retail therapy.

People seek various kinds of therapy when struggling with grief and loss. Many go for counseling while others prefer solitude. My initial response for that feel-good time in the midst of sadness was to eat.

Admittedly, I am not a health nut, so my food therapy consisted of chips, Diet Coke, Hostess CupCakes, Diet Coke, Micky D's french fries, Diet Coke, and Hostess CupCakes, followed by a Diet Coke.

Hostess CupCakes have long been one of my favorite junk foods, beginning when I was five and watched *The Howdy Doody Show* each afternoon. The host, Buffalo Bob, would tell the puppet, Howdy, how wonderful Hostess CupCakes were, and Howdy would often take a bite from one while Clarabell the Clown, Chief Thunderthud, and the Flubadub (a creature of unknown origin but with a taste for cupcakes as well) looked on. Buffalo Bob would, with the voice of a co-conspirator against the broccoli being offered by parents, tell us kids and Howdy to be sure to look for the secret surprise inside the cupcake. Howdy would nod his little wooden head in agreement. For years after my childhood indoctrination into the world of junk food, I always bit carefully into a Hostess CupCake, certain that the cream center would indeed be in the shape of some animal or toy. It's what Buffalo Bob and Howdy said. But, alas, my childhood innocence was shattered to find that the cream filling was just that—cream filling. The good news for me was that Hostess CupCakes remained one of those easily accessible junk foods requiring no preparation, whereas steamed broccoli did.

Some months after my haze of junk food therapy wore off and I realized I had gained twenty pounds, I took a long look at my life and the depths to which my grief had taken me. I started getting out more, I joined a few ladies' groups, and I worked on losing the extra twenty pounds. I read my daily Bible devotionals and sang the hymns in church with a bit more fervor and fewer moments of needing a handkerchief. However, one vice I had developed during those darker days remained. Perhaps it was there all along, even before the Captain's death, but now I used it to lift my spirits and act as a deterrent to Hostess CupCakes. Retail therapy became my go-to source of solitary enjoyment. I loved to shop for clothes.

Please understand that I didn't have to buy clothes. I just liked wandering around, looking, trying things on, and, if the price was from the red tag sale, I might make a purchase. I'm not sure for whom I wanted to look nice since Max was gone and as a woman in her late sixties, I doubt seriously anyone else was looking. Perhaps I just wanted to see myself in a way that didn't reflect the sadness that I knew was etched across my face. Or maybe I wanted to reinvent myself after becoming a single person following so many years of being a couple. Whatever the reason, wandering in shops and through stores made me smile until a young woman in one shop showed me the folly of my "therapy."

I entered Classy Clothes and Jewelry on the town square, with the dainty shop bell announcing my arrival. I heard what I thought was "good morning" from behind the sales desk. I looked up to see a figure hunched over a cell phone, texting or maybe tweeting, chirping, squawking, or whatever people do on their phones these days. No matter what she was doing, I could have been a three-headed snake (from my art room and my nightmares) and she would not have noticed. Bright pink streaks ran through her dark-brown hair, and the reason for the mumbled greeting appeared to be the three small silver rings that dangled from her upper lip. Enhancing the beauty of the embellished lip, she had two silver studs impaling both sides of her nose and a number of silver earrings so vast I lost count; I wondered if perhaps she herself was the jewelry display case. Adding further to her creative self-decoration was a silver navel ring, which I could clearly see because she had mistakenly put on her little sister's tank top that morning, leaving her midriff bare. As a final adornment and in an obvious attempt to match her hair streaks, was the tattoo of a bright pink unicorn on her right shoulder.

When she opened her mouth to ask if she could help me—this was done without ever looking up and with fingers still flying across her phone—I was greatly relieved to see that her mumbled welcome wasn't difficult for me to understand because I needed a hearing aid but rather because of the large metal stud penetrating her tongue and the chewing

21

gum filling her mouth. Texting, tweeting, mumbling, and chewing gum all at the same time struck me as the modern version of multitasking, to say nothing about the extra weight she was carrying from the supplemental metal on her person. I could not imagine her ever getting through a TSA checkpoint at the airport.

Unlike this girl, I was twenty-eight years old before I ever got my ears pierced. Perhaps my delay in body piercing was because my mother had ingrained in me that "nice" girls didn't get their ears pierced. And once I had convinced Mother that I *was* a nice girl, she used the old "If you get into a fight with another girl, she might rip your earring out, and what boy would want to date you or marry you with a torn earlobe?" excuse. Truth be told, I never got into a physical altercation with anyone other than my older sister and that stopped at about the age of seven. The real reason I delayed getting my ears pierced is that I abhor pain. It didn't take a mental giant to know that sticking needles through your earlobes would hurt. Can you imagine the look of shock on the face of the clerk at the piercing salon when I told her she'd have to use two piercing guns and do both ears at the same time? I knew that if I ever let her do one ear, I'd *never* let her do the other. It was obvious that the shop girl currently before me had no mother to instill irrational terror in her heart and that she was immune to pain.

Turning away from my obvious wonderment that someone would so decorate her body, metallurgically speaking, I wandered toward the clothing racks when I heard an additional mumble, "We don't carry anything larger than a size nine."

That stopped me cold! I immediately walked out of the shop and reread its name to make sure I hadn't made a mistake. It still read Classy Clothing and Jewelry and I wondered how the young lady knew I wasn't there to buy a scarf, a handbag, or a piece of jewelry from the *regular* display counter. The obvious answer was that she didn't, so I marched myself back in to do battle with Lady Metallica, stating that size nine was just my size, and proceeding to pull stacks of clothes off the racks, I walked determinedly into the dressing room.

I recognized that my days of being a size nine were long past, but the young lady's presumption that I *wasn't* a size nine rankled me, especially since she still had not looked up from her phone. I tried on piece after piece, to my heart's content, knowing they wouldn't fit but enjoying the discomfiture of the salesgirl when I poked my head out of the dressing room and asked her to get me the next size smaller in a particular garment. I kept up the assault on most of the size nines in the store until the dressing room was littered with hangers, price tags, and the occasional size seven. I then did something that *would* make my mother think I wasn't so nice after all: I left all those classy clothes strewn about the dressing room and walked out.

As I left, I looked back over my shoulder and remarked to the salesclerk that none of the clothes were classy enough for my discerning taste and sweetly suggested she might think about changing her hair streak from bright pink to a gray-blue to better match her silver. I fear she was stuck with the pink unicorn. And with my head held high, I walked around the corner to the donut shop and had a Bavarian cream chocolate-covered donut. It wasn't a Hostess CupCake, but it came close.

Being a size nine or a five or a two is a distant memory. My body appears to like my current weight since nothing I do seems to move the needle on the scale. Amazingly, I had a husband who always saw me as the size five I was on our first date. But without his validating comments, I have had to learn that I am still the same person he loved and, more importantly, whom God loves, regardless of how I look or what I wear. For the reader, it may be that the job you lost defined you or that the marriage that crumbled was a reflection of who you were to the rest of the world. But the truth of what God sees *in* us rather than what the world sees is the real measure of a life well lived.

And what about the young salesclerk? I saw someone who looked different from me, someone who had tastes different than mine, and also someone who, like me, appeared to think how she looked defined who she was. Sadly, in my moment of trying to cope with my loss, I forgot that she could be just as worthy of God's love as you or I. Though she seemed to show me no regard, my actions had exemplified that same attitude of disrespect. Seeking God's love and forgiveness is a greater goal than deference or even worldly respect, and I pray that this goal will lead me to show more compassion to others, regardless of how they look, dress, or speak, what job they hold, or their marital status.

When I step on the scale and look at the unmoving numbers, my mind is drawn to the truth that we should not "boast about outward appearance" but rather "about what is in our heart" (2 Corinthians 5:12). As I sit at my desk, looking out of my window, I see the lovely irises a friend shared with me from her garden and marvel at the beauty God created on this earth. I know, too, that God is looking at the beauty within the hearts of His creations, and when He does, I pray He sees a size XXXL in us all.

Reflections:

1. What do you do when you've had a terrible day? A horrible month? A devastating year? Read Matthew 6:9–13, Romans 8:18, 26–28.

2. What causes stress in your life? Read Matthew 11:29.

3. What are your favorite means of coping?

4. Are your coping strategies actions that would be pleasing to God? If not, what are some ways in which you might change those strategies? Read 1John 3:19–24.

"Casting all your anxieties on Him because He cares for you."

1 Peter 5:7

CHAPTER 4

"Don't You Just Love It When a Plan Comes Together"

"Face" from *The A-Team*

"The heart of a man plans his way, but the LORD establishes his steps."

Proverbs 16:9

The other afternoon, as I was trying to convince myself to use one of my four vacuum cleaners, the movie, *The A-Team* came on TV and provided me with the perfect excuse not to vacuum. While I remembered Max and me watching the long-running TV show with George Peppard and Mr. T, I also recalled that we thoroughly enjoyed the updated movie version. Though the actors had changed, the general complexion of the team had not: Murdock was still the deranged but hilarious pilot, B.A. was still afraid of flying, Faceman still got the girl, and Colonel "Hannibal" Smith still held the team together as they devised ingenious, "explosive" plans to save the day. My husband never failed to delight in the often-repeated line, "Don't you just love it when a plan comes together" because he knew the plan would be outlandish, dangerous, improbable, yet successful.

Sometimes the plans we make for our lives mirror that sense of the incredible, improbable, and outlandish, but make plans we do. I suppose what keeps us making these plans is the belief that we control all that happens in our lives—that we have things well in hand—that we know best. These self-made plans are often reflected on my calendar where I plot out what I will do each day. Whether vacuuming, lunching with a friend, keeping appointments, or watching outlandish movies on TV, I am a planner. I am also a list maker. Max would often see me head off to the market, only to return minutes later because I had forgotten my list. And if the Captain were going with me, the list became even more critical; if he had just followed the items on my list, we never would have ended up with Vienna sausages, jalapeños stuffed with tuna, Spam, and other oddities. It isn't any wonder that our oldest son grew up to be a planner as well.

Some time ago, Patrick came up with The Plan to buy a new car. That might not sound unusual except that it was to be a surprise for his wife, Rachel, who was out of town. Instead, The Plan involved me and read as follows: 1) Mom travels from Oxford, Mississippi, to Minden, Louisiana; 2) Mom accompanies Patrick to Shreveport, Louisiana, in the old car; 3) two grandchildren are strapped in car seats in the back of the old car and plied with fruit snacks and Capri Sun during travel; 4) Patrick drops Mom and the Grands at nearby Chick-fil-A while Patrick continues to the car dealership; 5) Mom is to have a pleasant, quiet breakfast with the Grands until Patrick's return with the new car; 6) family travels safely back to Minden in the new car; 7) Rachel is happily surprised when she returns home. All went as planned until #5 exploded, much like a scene from *The A-Team*.

The arrangement for breakfast at Chick-fil-A was not a bad idea. The children loved it; they could chitchat with the large black-and-white cardboard cow, they liked the breakfast menu, and, should the need arise, they would obligingly use the bathroom because it was equipped with old-fashioned manual flushing toilets that did not commence flushing automatically, often before the task was completed! Number 5 of The Plan did not, however, have an addendum that *should have read*: Mom does not allow the Grands anywhere near the room with a child-sized hamster habitat in it.

Many fast-food restaurants now contain areas of play for children, but we have come a long way from the simple pool of plastic balls at the local Mickey D's. Fast-food restaurants have graduated to a maze of tubes and slides housed in a room separate from the eating area. Shoes are removed and signage points out that no one over the age of eight is allowed in the play area. The play zones always seemed vaguely familiar, in a rodent sort of way. I have long suspected that the designers of these play zones had worked in pet stores prior to their design work for restaurants.

Admittedly, I had not been in a pet store for many years. My last occasion to enter such a shop was when a woman came running from one, screaming, "They're spinning the gerbils." I was close enough to the store to look in and see three familiar heads leaning over a box filled with a minia-ture Ferris wheel and small furry creatures. The heads belonged to my two sons, Patrick and Ryan, and their best friend, James. As I inched closer, I saw Patrick put one of the small furry creatures on the bottom of the Ferris wheel. Then all three boys, with hands on the wheel, counted "one, two, three" and spun the wheel as hard as they could. The net result was that centrifugal force kept the small furry creature within the wheel for about two revolutions, at which point it fell out and dizzily staggered around the large, boxed area. The boys found this to be hilarious. The store manage-ment did not, and we were banished from the pet store forever.

To be fair, our boys never gave any of the gerbils more than a sin-gle ride on the Ferris wheel, and their actions actually helped the store to increase its sales of the plastic habitat tubing. I'm convinced that no gerbil or hamster or any member of the rodent family was seriously hurt in these experiments, but our names and faces were posted on the front of the store by PETA as a warning to other potential "gerbil spinners." My embarrassment led to an intense dislike of hamster habitats. To compound this aversion, the boys and I were further traumatized by what we found when touring a prospective house to purchase in Virginia where we saw the "mother" of all hamster habitats in the middle of the family room floor.

The boys, fresh off their banishment from the pet store, rushed over to see the critters in their "hands off" environment, only to find they were all dead. I mean, they were stiff as boards–five of them–all on their little rodent backs with their little rodent feet in the air. I remember Max comforted the boys, offering words of solace and ending with a phrase that said it all: "Now their little moccasins are to the moon." I think he got that phrase from the Indian Y Guide handbook, and the boys readily accepted that the will of the Great Chief in the Sky had been done.

We did not buy the house.

Now, so many years after the Hamster Death House incident, here I was facing a "hamster habitat" once again and this time the Grands wanted to be the hamsters. Lela Margaret was four, and Treat was three. I did not meet the eight years of age restriction. Both children scampered up the tubes, right to the top, and waved cheerily to me below. They played around the tubes and tunnels for some time before Lela Margaret joyfully slid down the attached slide with a high-pitched "Wheeeee!" I waited patiently for Treat to do the same. And waited . . . and waited.

Treat was still waving to me from the top-most part of the "habitat," but the happy wave from moments earlier had become gestures of panic. I smiled to encourage him. "Slide down, Treat."

His reply was more frantic waving.

Lela Margaret tugged on my skirt. "Treat doesn't do slides."

I pulled out my printed copy of The Plan. Nowhere did it say, "Rescue child from giant hamster habitat." My attempt to send Lela Margaret back up the tubes to help Treat was met with typical sibling disdain. Captain Max, being the engineer that he was, would have come up with a rescue plan worthy of The A-Team, but I did the only thing I could. Ignoring the eight-year-old age limit, I took off my shoes and crawled up the tube.

The Plan not only failed to mention saving small children but also did not include instructions for wearing slacks rather than a skirt. I can firmly attest that a mature woman, wearing a skirt and climbing up tubing made for the size of a child, while trying to maintain any modesty was a herculean task, and dignity was out of the question.

When I finally got to Treat, I tried to coerce him into climbing back down with me, but to no avail. That left the slide as our only means of escape. Deciding to put Treat in my lap and just slide down was a sound plan had it not been for my hips, which were wedged so tightly into the child-sized slide that we didn't budge. We just sat at the top with Lela Margaret below yelling, "Come on down! Come on down!"

Ankles firmly crossed in my most ladylike position, I inched our way down, with each inch making a squeaky sound and the necessary repositioning of my skirt as it rode up my ample hips. Three agonizing minutes later, I made it to ground zero. Everyone in the restaurant cheered, the children hugged me, and Treat looked up to me with pleading eyes. "Can we do it again?"

"No, it's not in your father's plan!" And we waited outside for the new car and driver.

The plan I had for my life did not include losing Max in a car accident just as we were nearing the age where we could rest on our laurels and begin to enjoy the life of retirees. We had planned to travel. We had planned to help our grandchildren with college. We had even planned to have the granddaughters' wedding receptions in our backyard, though at the time, none were over the age of six. But those were our plans, not God's plans.

Our human minds are too small to comprehend the immensity of God's plans for our lives. Like Job in the Bible, we often pray the "why" rather than admitting our limitations to fully understand God's plans. God doesn't mind that we ask why, but in asking, we must be ready to accept His answer.

Accepting God's sovereignty in our lives is one of the most difficult aspects of living, especially when faced with a sudden loss, because it means giving up our control and our plans to someone else. But God isn't *just* someone else. He is the Creator, who made me and knew me even when I was in my mother's womb. And because God is wholly and completely good, I cannot help but believe that whatever plans He has for my life will *ultimately* be good.

By "good" I do not mean a life without pain and suffering. After all, we live in a world that has been made imperfect by sin, and sin carries consequences. But what does one consider the term *good* to mean?

For me, its meaning becomes clear by following the handiwork of God throughout the scriptures and seeing the way in which He deals with the lives of His people in this sin-filled world. The book of Genesis uses the word *good* to describe God's glorious creation, including mankind, and according to *Strongs Concordance*, it is translated from Hebrew as "favorable or beneficial." Matthew 19:17 says, "No one is good but One, that is God."[5] Here again, though written many centuries later, *good* still translates as beneficial but its meaning is expanded, and *Strong's Concordance* now defines *good* as meaning "morally and honorably beneficial."[5] And we know from Psalm 23 that the goodness of God can overcome evil.

Loss that brings pain is an evil with which we all must cope. We plan against loss and the evils of this world but those plans, however well laid out, are imperfect because they are our plans in *this* world. But God is not of this world. He is that morally and honorable father who offers benefits to us, His wayward children. Because He is good, sadness, sorrow and evil can be overcome. He is perfect and His blueprints reflect considerations we cannot fathom.

One can only imagine the questions people put to God: *Will I get Alzheimer's like my mother did? Why does my spouse want a divorce? Why did I get passed over for the job? How much longer will I be able to climb a ladder? Why did my husband have to die? Why does my child have cancer?*

Circumstances in our lives will always lead us to ask "why" because we are flawed human beings, but we must remember that while God has the answer to that question, our question may, for a time, be answered with silence. God knows the time and place where we will all be able to fully understand His plan–that we will one day look back and see a divine guidance in the life we have lived.

The inerrant plan of God is clearly seen in the story of Joseph who went to live in Egypt after his brothers sold him into slavery and where he would become the person who could save his family from starvation. "I am Joseph! Now do not be distressed or angry with yourselves because you sold me here, for God sent me before you to preserve life" (Genesis 45:3, 5). Joseph clearly believed in the sovereignty of God and His plans.

Acceptance is not easy to achieve if the sovereignty of God is not etched firmly on your heart. Yet the Bible tells us repeatedly about the depth of God's love for us and His desire to bless us abundantly. One may not see a loss as a blessing, but I know somehow it is. The purely good God loves me so much that He sent Christ, His only Son, to the cross for me so that His plan for my life would end in joy beyond measure with assurances to last a lifetime.

Reflections:

1. What does the term "sovereignty of God" mean to you?

2. What plans have you made recently that had an unexpected outcome? Were you upset or pleased with the outcome?

3. How far ahead do you make plans?

4. Do you seek God's guidance through prayer before making plans? Read Matthew 6:33.

5. List three times when your life did not go as planned. How did you react to those changes?

6. Could you see God at work in those unplanned outcomes? Read Hosea 14:9.

"As for you, you meant evil against me but God meant it for good."

Genesis 50:20

CHAPTER 5

Driving Miss Crazy

"For the law was given through Moses; grace
and truth came through Jesus Christ."

John1:17

I got cussed out at the McDonald's drive-thru yesterday. Max would have told me that my first mistake was *going* to the drive-thru!

As we got older, I noticed the Captain increasingly avoided the drive-thrus and instead gallantly leaped from the car to go in and get me my requisite Diet Coke. For a while, I believed that he wanted to make sure he got the proportions of ice to drink just right, which touched my heart. However, I eventually learned that all of my teasing Max about needing Miracle-Ear had more truth to it than tease. Like so many people our age, his hearing was waning, though one doctor he consulted told him it was only the tone of *my* voice he couldn't hear. But I discounted that rather chauvinistic diagnosis as I stopped to review the way Max spoke when we did go through the drive-thru:

Kind Employee: May I help you?

Captain: YES . . . I . . . WOULD . . . LIKE . . . A . . . LARGE . . . DIET . . . COKE . . . THAT'S . . . ALL . . . THANK . . . YOU (Spoken at about 200 decibels).

Kind Employee: Will that complete your order?

Captain: NO . . . I . . . JUST . . . WANT . . . A . . . LARGE . . . DIET . . . COKE . . . . THANK . . . YOU.

Kind Employee: So, it's only a Diet Coke, correct? Your total is a dollar and nine cents.

Captain: NO . . . I . . . DON'T . . . WANT . . . ANY . . . FRIES . . . THANK . . . YOU.

Kind Employee: Why don't you just drive through, sir, and we'll figure it out when you get to the window.

Captain: HELLO! . . . IS . . . ANYBODY . . . THERE? . . . DID . . . YOU . . . GET . . . MY . . . ORDER?

At this point, I'd nudge him, and although I don't know American Sign Language, he usually understood that my frantic movements meant he should drive on through to the window.

But driving on through is exactly what got me into trouble today as I innocently pulled into the single line at Micky D's in search of my Diet Coke fix. Only two cars were in front of me, one of which was at the deciding point, that spot where the line of cars goes from one lane to two. Suddenly, there was movement, and the driver of the lead car, a black sedan, turned into the lower inside lane, pulling next to the ordering squawk box. However, the car directly in front of me ignored all drive-thru protocol and did not move an inch. Max might have said she was frozen in "drive-thru hell," unable to make that earth-shattering decision as to which lane to take. Ironically, for me, and for the six cars behind me, the upper lane was empty and had been since I'd first arrived. It seemed like the obvious choice for lane selection.

While I have never been as polite as my husband always was, I did understand about waiting my turn and that the unwritten rule of *no cuts* applied to the lines at fast-food restaurants just as it did to movie theaters, Disneyland, and the ladies' bathroom at sporting events. So, I waited and waited, all the while listening to the motors revving behind me as other patrons tried to adhere to the *no cuts* rule as well.

Finally, when I could see that the line behind me reached all the way back to the street and that no more cars could enter the drive-thru lane, I decided I had to take a stand. I mean, there's the *no cuts* rule, but there is also the rule that you should get off your phone, pay attention to life and the pursuit of happiness, which for me was getting a Diet Coke. I considered honking, but Max had trained me never to do that out of anger or frustration, both emotions at work in me at that moment. I went back to my old stand-by of gesturing wildly since it had always worked so well with the Captain, but to no avail. The car ahead would not budge. I caved to the revving engines behind me and bravely drove to the empty upper lane. Three cars followed. I arrived at the squawk box, ready to order.

A sudden, loud bang snapped me out of my sense of vehicular leadership, and I quickly realized that the sound was the slamming of a car door followed by screaming. The driver from "the car that would not move" had exited her vehicle and was stopping at each of the cars that had followed when I had blazed the trail to the upper lane. She was gesturing wildly and yelling at each of the drivers behind me. Arriving at my car, she said, "You have to wait your turn."

"I waited for quite a long time, but you never moved," I replied.

She crossed her arms over her chest and sneered at me. "Drive-thru etiquette demands that one wait until the right front tire is on the yellow line that starts the division of the drive-thru lanes before making the lane choice." She pointed to said yellow line. "My right front tire has not yet touched that line!"

I considered telling her that the reason she had not reached the dividing line was that one actually had to put the car into "drive" to be able to move ahead. Instead, I held my tongue and rolled up my window. With my window up, I could still hear her screaming that I'd have to exit and go to the end of the line. I knew this to be an impossibility since she had not moved her car, and it continued to block the single drive-thru lane, which was still backed up to the street; no one could enter. While she called me foul names and shouted and gestured at those other drive-thru hoodlums behind me, I suddenly realized I'd forgotten to order my Diet Coke.

I surreptitiously rolled down my window and yelled at the speaker, "I'd like a large Diet Coke. Thank you." I did not wait to hear my order repeated, nor did I wait to hear the total, and I certainly didn't take the time to ask for fries. I just raced to the payment window, where I could still hear the screams of a woman driven to the brink of madness by the simple convenience of not having to get out of her car to order. The Captain would have said it was a sign of end times, but I just muttered, "What a way to start the day."

The woman who became irrationally enraged at the McDonald's drive-thru certainly started my day off on a bad note. She was so angry at the alleged affront by those of us who moved the line forward that she failed to look at the underlying cause—her inattentiveness. Her anger truly startled me and became the catalyst for my thoughts for the rest of the day.

I am a rule follower by nature. I admittedly count people's grocery items in the ten-items-or-less lane. I keep track of when a waiter takes my order and delivers my meal in relation to the other customers who may have ordered *after* me. I suppose my worst and most dangerous attempt at forcing life's rules on others is when I see a sign announcing that, due to construction, the road is closing to a single lane, whereupon I drive down the middle of the road to keep other motorists from zooming ahead to get in front of me instead of waiting their turn. Sounds an awful lot like the woman at McDonald's, doesn't it?

God set down rules for how mankind should live. Some rules helped to direct a safe and just society. Some were ordained to keep our bodies healthy, and some were to keep our minds pure. Still others were to bring us into closer communion with God. Thus, mankind began to follow these rules, but because mankind is inherently sinful, even the ways in which humans followed God's laws became corrupted. A good example is the way in which the Pharisees of Jesus' time would pray loudly and frequently, but more for recognition of their actions than as a means of communicating with the Lord (Luke 18:11). Taken to extremes, the Pharisees became judgmental; they took the rules God set down for all mankind and manipulated them to enhance their power over the children of Israel, becoming conceited, obstinate, and overly critical of all others in the process. They were ruled by the sin of pride and allowed it to fill every facet of their relationship with God, letting everyone know *they followed the rules.*

But what about those of us that know and love the rules but just can't seem to follow them at all times? Are we sure to fail because we disappoint God? Is there some grand work we can go out and specifically do to make up for our failings? Are we doomed because we are imperfect?

Starting with the birth of a babe in Bethlehem, God laid all those broken rules at the foot of the Cross. The Savior's blood dripped down and covered all those shattered laws and offered, instead, a life filled with grace. The Lord knows the measure of a person by his love for God and the goodness in his heart. By believing in the sacrifice made by Christ, the Holy Spirit fills believers with a desire to work through that sin, uplifting those rules to become second nature and God-approved. We are saved by grace and not by a recitation of the rules; we look to Christ, not the rulebook, so that we live "to do justice, and to love kindness, and to walk humbly with your God" (Micah 6:8).

Christ clothes us with His righteousness and extends to us a chance to live with Him forever, where grief from death, loss, personal conflict or disappointment will be no more. And the laws we follow will be because of our love for Christ and His for us, rather than the rulebook.

Reflections:

1. Are you a rule follower?

2. What are your thoughts about someone who does not follow the rules but still seems to get ahead in life? Read Micah 6:8 and Proverbs 22:4.

3. What does it mean "to do justice?" Read Deuteronomy 32:4, Proverbs 12:5, and Matthew 5:45.

4. What does it mean to "love kindness?" Read Proverbs 21:21, Roman 11:22, and Ephesians 4:31–32.

5. What does it mean to "walk humbly?" Read Matthew 23:12, Philippians 2:3–8 and Proverbs 11:2.

6. How might your life change by "privately and prayerfully" following Micah 6:8? Do you think your attempt to live by Micah 6:8 would be done because of an increased desire to please God or so you could declare yourself "good?"

"Now the law came to increase the trespass but where sin increased, grace abounded all the more, so that as sin reigned in death, grace might also reign through righteousness, leading to eternal life through Jesus Christ, our Lord."

Romans 5:20–21

CHAPTER 6

"Indian Love Call"

From Rose Marie by Sigmund Romberg

"Then our mouth was filled with laughter and our tongue with shouts of joy; and they said among the nations, 'The LORD has done great things for them,' The LORD has done great things for us; we are glad."

Psalm 126:2

After my husband was killed, I was asked to join a literary society. A sweet older lady from a local church invited me, and when I arrived at the first meeting, I discovered that most of the members were widows or single women who outranked me in age by at least twenty years. I immediately thought, *boring, boring, boring!* I could not have been more wrong.

The club had the catchy name of the Ladies Literary Society, so named because Miss Eula Mae Thompson decreed it. Ramrod straight with an old-fashioned bun at the nape of her long neck, Miss Eula Mae wore sufficient Pan-Cake makeup to keep Max Factor in business for the next hundred years or until she passed from this life, something Miss Eula Mae declared would never happen. Her eyes were a piercing blue, her nose came to an aquiline point, and her eyebrows were in a permanent position that suggested she questioned the sanity of all others in her presence. For a moment, I was in awe of her, but later decided it was abject terror when I realized she reminded me of my first-grade teacher who had been known to tie small children to the leg of her desk or lock them in the broom closet.

Seated next to Miss Eula Mae—yes, we were required to call her "Miss" at all times, though she was known to have had three husbands— was Lettie Amberton. Petite with salt-and-pepper hair, Lettie's demure attitude would never allow her to raise her eyes above the string of pearls that rested on Miss Eula Mae's ample bosom. Lettie was the league's *scribe*, which I would have called the secretary, but Miss Eula Mae said that *scribe* sounded so much more literary.

Across the table from Lettie were the Schneider twins, Mildred and Myrtle. They were identical in every way, from their dyed red beehive hair-dos to their scarves tied coquettishly around the plentiful folds of their necks, to their Chuck Taylor pink high-top tennis shoes. Once upon a time, the Schneider twins had been high school librarians who gained a repu-tation for roaming the stacks on roller skates, seeking out those students who might have been inspired to *act* out Shakespeare's love sonnets rather than just reading them. Not caring about the *Silence Please* sign that the twins, themselves, had posted, Mildred and Myrtle were said to have bor-rowed whistles from the football coach and used them liberally when roll-ing past would-be Romeos and Juliettes. The twins were active members of DatesWanted.com.

When I realized that the twins had left their football whistles at home, I began to relax and took my seat next to Madge Rutledge, the lady who had invited me. Madge was tall and willowy, wearing tailored trousers, sensible Oxfords, and a messy bun held together by two #2 pencils on the tip-top of her head. She had the most genteel way of speaking, melodious to the ear, and such a dynamic difference from the raucous laughter of the twins or the imperious disdain that clung to every word uttered by Miss Eula Mae.

Rounding out our merry little band was Lucy Overbeck, professor emeritus of English Literature, who, I think, was asleep, because of her head resting on her chest and the quiet yet audible snores that emanated from her slightly open mouth. I couldn't see her eyes to be absolutely sure as her coke-bottle glasses made her eyes appear as watery blurs. Madge passed me a note under the table that read: "I've diagnosed it as narcolepsy, but it could be boredom." Madge's late husband had been a doctor, and she spent many afternoons pouring over his old medical books. I soon discovered that she would, at one time or another, offer diagnoses to each of us, except for Miss Eula Mae, who, like Mary Poppins, was practically perfect.

Thanksgiving was near, and with thoughts of that legendary first meal shared by Pilgrims and Native Americans, Miss Eula Mae decreed that we would study an Iroquois Indian prayer. Melding her love of the Greek classics with Native American literature seemed either daring or something suggested by the Schneider twins, and we were instructed to read the Iroquois prayer in the format of a Greek chorus, with Miss Eula Mae being the head Greek. Just as Miss Eula Mae began her oration, Lucy Overbeck woke up long enough to ask what the date for the Literary League Christmas party was.

I now fully understand the phrase *rose up* because that is what Miss Eula Mae did. She seemed to have levitated from her seat at the head of the table and shot Lucy a look that would have withered the mighty oak about to be described in the Iroquois prayer. The look, however withering, was to no avail as Lucy's head had slumped back to her chest, followed by a loud snore. Roused to defend their slumbering comrade, other members of the League clamored to know about the Christmas party as well.

Miss Eula Mae, still levitating and withering, firmly announced that we were reading the Iroquois Prayer of Thanksgiving and the discussion of parties was out of order. Unfortunately, Miss Eula Mae had not counted on the other members of the League being party animals. The discussion of the Christmas party could be heard over the stentorian sound of "Great

Spirit of the forest, we offer our thanks for the plentiful hunting and the ripened stalks of the corn."

Amazingly, maybe even a little frighteningly, with no one paying any attention to Miss Eula Mae's talking points of lodges, tribal councils, and arrowheads, she suddenly stopped, and with a voice as cold as icicles, said, "The party will be hosted by Madge, as always."

Lettie cried out that she never got to host the party. Mildred and Myrtle suggested that the party be held at the local roller-skating rink. Madge said *she didn't want* to host the party anymore. Lucy snored. I kept my mouth shut.

I came to discover that Madge had, indeed, always hosted the party, but she had done it as a reluctant co-hostess with Theresa Nuzoni, who was wealthy, dripping with furs, jewels, and silver, and by this time, quite dead. In Madge's defense for not wanting to co-host the annual fete, it turned out that Theresa Nuzoni's husband had been the local bootlegger, whose ill-gotten gains had kept Theresa in the furs, the jewels, and the silver. Madge claimed she always feared that declining to cohost with Theresa would be consigning herself to cement boots á la Jimmy Hoffa rather than her sensible Oxfords. Mr. Nuzoni had gone on to his greater reward, having succumbed to too much of his own product, and while Madge no longer needed to fear the Italian's retribution, she claimed she often still dreamed of being made an offer she "couldn't refuse." Unlike the untimely death of Mr. Nuzoni, Theresa lived to be 103 and attended church each Sunday morning, always sitting in the second row from the front. Her hair never changed from its ink bottle black, with eyebrows to match and perfect bow-shaped lips in bright red. And regardless of the weather, a dead, furry animal was always draped around her shoulders. The jewels and silver completed her look until the day she died.

Ignoring the discussion of boot-legged whiskey and dead furry animals and still giving thanks to the Iroquois, Miss Eula Mae suddenly raised her arms to the skies, increasing her volume, and in a loud reverent voice said, "Thank you, Great Spirit, for the many colors of the season and fragrant aromas carried on the autumn breezes."

Lucy awoke to suggest that the aroma was probably smoke from peyote and the colors were those of a psychedelic trip. An argument ensued among the League members as to whether it was the Iroquois or the Plains Indians who used peyote in their rituals. By then, Miss Eula Mae was tearing her script into tiny little pieces; Madge suggested that the mafia was involved in the decimation of the Native Americans; Lettie announced the date of the Christmas party at *her* house and the Schneider twins offered to bring onion dip and roller skates. And after picking myself up off the floor where I had fallen, bent over double, hysterically laughing, I walked out of my first meeting of the Ladies Literary League still laughing and assured that if I had to grow old alone after the loss of my husband, I would henceforth strive to discover more about Native Americans and their rich culture, learn to roller skate, and never forget that humor is all around me, even if it's brought on by ninety-year-old comedians.

Sarah laughed! And like the ladies of the Literary League, she was in her nineties. How could people in their nineties, as she and Abraham both were, bring forth a child, let alone care for one (Genesis 18:12–15; 21:6)? But with God, all things are possible. He is the God who had promised Abraham and Sarah they would have a child, and Isaac was born. God kept His promise!

One may ask how those of us who carry the burden of great loss can laugh. The honest answer is that many times we can't. Even when we do laugh, the sense of loss is still there, sometimes accompanied by a sense of guilt because we momentarily forgot to be sad. Indeed, Proverbs 14:13 says, "Even in laughter the heart may ache, and the end of joy may be grief."

However, C.S. Lewis' book, *Mere Christianity,* helps us to understand that as we try to embrace joy and laughter, even when it's hard to do so, we will eventually see that same joy and laughter become part of our daily lives: "There is also (pretending), a good kind where the pretense leads up

47

to the real thing." Lewis continues to explain that "often the only way to get a quality in reality is to start behaving as if you already had it."[3] Thus, by exhibiting a joyful attitude, one may actually begin to find that joy is fully present again.

Jesus reminds us that joy is part of the process of living and healing. He doesn't say that we will forget what makes us weep or mourn. However, He does tell us that He understands our sorrow, and that our sorrow will eventually give way to joy when we come before His presence: "So also you have sorrow now, but I will see you again, and in your hearts will rejoice, and no one will take your joy from you" (John 16:22).

It is with hope that we can let the day come when, for a moment, we forget our loss, find joy, and laugh– not because the loss isn't still with us, but because God has added a dimension to our day when His joyous spirit will overshadow the darkness of loss. When we least expect it, He will surround us with joy, laughter and life.

Reflections:

1. Do you think laughter is part of the healing process? If so, how? Read John 15:11

2. Do you actively seek to find joyful moments when coping with loss? Do you experience a sense of guilt when those moments come? If so, why? Read Isaiah 55:12 and Ecclesiastes 3:1–8.

3. Can you laugh at yourself?

4. Do you think God laughs? If so, at what?

"Blessed are those who weep for now you shall laugh."

Luke 6:21b

CHAPTER 7

"The Flowers That Bloom in the Spring, Tra La"

From *The Mikado*, Gilbert and Sullivan

"...and be content with what you have, for he said,
"I will never leave you or forsake you."

Hebrews 13:5

Living in a small southern town has taught me many things that I'd never have learned if had I stayed in my home state of California. And I suppose one of the most important things is that the mayor, the aldermen, and the board of supervisors are not the real power brokers in a southern town. True absolute power is genteelly wielded by women bearing pruning shears, carrying spray guns of insecticide, and carting the occasional watering can. Yes, I am talking about the ladies of the local Garden Club, who, to date, have *not* asked me to join.

The members I know in this very select organization are usually soft-spoken, emitting the perfect southern persona of strength through sweetness. They have successfully disguised their wills of iron and have used negotiating skills that would make them powerful assets at the United Nations. These ladies know what they want for the community. Using their deceptively sweet influence on the local administrators, they bring about an agenda, which, in their estimation, is what the community needs. They get it done and done to perfection.

It's important to understand that I was not necessarily Garden Club material. Our house plants languished due to neglect or because our cat kept eating them. Outdoor gardening had always been something to avoid, like Brussels sprouts, broccoli, and sushi. Digging in the ground would have required contact with earthworms, grasshoppers, and the ever-present snakes. I shudder at the mere thought.

And though digging in the ground might not appeal to me, being asked to join the most powerful group in town seemed a natural fit. At Bakersfield High School, I proudly carried the nickname Janis Join-All. During my junior and senior years, I held the record for the most pictures in my high school annual. Later in life, I served as PTA president for three straight years, oversaw the Officers' Wives Club as president long before it became the Officers' Spouses Club, nurtured boys into young men as Cub Scout Coordinator, and my renown as the four-term advisor to the Junior-Senior Prom for Long Beach High School reached monumental proportions all along the Mississippi Gulf Coast.

Unfortunately, not only hadn't my renown as a power broker spread to North Mississippi, but the Oxford Garden Club had a requirement I could not meet: the ability to grow plants. I think somewhere in their rules of membership was a phrase that euthanizing house plants of any kind, herbaceous cats notwithstanding, would be grounds for immediate expulsion.

Never one to run from a challenge, I filled out my application for membership based on my one and only positive experience with plant life. I hoped that the committee would be very impressed with my efforts at "floral preservation" as I recounted how I successfully faced and defeated a garden pest the likes of which had never been known in the annuals of the Oxford Garden Club. My application contained the following story:

When we were stationed in Anchorage, Alaska, I quickly discovered that outdoor gardening was a short-lived season but one that, in two short months, displayed all the floral beauty and variety normally seen in the South for nine months. People in Alaska went out of their way to enjoy the glory of God's creation on every downtown street corner and front porch, with the most spectacular displays being the hanging baskets of fuchsias.

Never in my life had I attempted to grow fuchsias, and my time in Alaska was no different. I just went to the store and bought them. And because it was August–technically the end of the growing season since we'd already had our first snow– my fuchsias were on the scrawny side, having been the last two at the store. But, as with most problems, if you throw enough money at it, *it* can be overcome. This meant that I took my two scrawny, nearly dead fuchsias to the local nursery to be repotted and wintered indoors for the small sum of $125 *per plant*; it's just what you did in Alaska. I can clearly remember my husband questioning the logic of spending that kind of money for two plants that had, together, cost a grand total of $11.99. But, as in so many instances, resignation spread across his face, followed by laughter. "My wife was an English Literature major, so what does she know about comparative finances?"

When the day arrived the following May for us to pick up the fuchsias, even Max was shocked at the magnificence of the plants, so obviously having been cared for during the nine months of winter by someone other than his wife. Word of their magnificence spread throughout the neighborhood and into the surrounding community of Anchorage. Amazingly, people assumed I had a hand in this magnificence, which led to a call from the president of the Anchorage Garden Club. Suddenly, I was up for membership, and my "fuchsias extraordinaire" were placed on the annual Garden Club Tour. I burst with pride!

Husband, Max, and son, Ryan, with their loving indulgence in my botanical depravity, made sure that the lawn was mowed, the siding of the house was washed, and the hedges were trimmed, further enhancing the beauty of the hanging baskets of fuchsias. After a long day in the yard, which during the Alaskan summertime was a *very* long day, the Captain and Ryan went for a walk while I took a long soak in the tub.

As I soaked, I heard the phone ring, which I did not answer. It rang again, and then again. Deciding that my watery reverie had been ruined, I got out of the tub and stood by the phone, waiting for the fourth call that was sure to come. The call was from my neighbor who was passing along a message from husband and son: "Open the garage door so we can get in the house." Since they had left the front door unlocked, I failed to see the necessity of opening the overhead garage door but, ever the well-trained Captain's wife, I did. I stormed out of the open garage door, intending to give both of them a talking-to for interrupting my two-hour bath, but I couldn't find them.

Suddenly, two heads popped up from behind the neighbor's trash-cans, and my husband shouted warnings at me, coupled with frantic hand gestures. Ryan kept repeating the motion of a knife across his throat, making me think I had ignored the ringing phone for a bit too long and that they were extremely upset with me. Ryan's hand gestures then changed from the universal sign of death by knife to the throat to the universal sign of death by antlers to the belly. I turned to my left. There stood an enormous bull moose nibbling on my ticket into the garden club. The brave Captain and his "mate" burst from behind the trashcans, dragging me to safety, quickly closing the garage door, and thus saving me from what they assured me would have been death by moose.

My imminent death averted, we settled in for the night and readied ourselves for the next day's Garden Club Tour. Early the next morning, going out the front door for a last-minute check of the fuchsias, I discovered that the moose had not simply nibbled on my beloved plants. He had eaten the entire side of both, leaving a trail of moose "nuggets" throughout my freshly manicured yard! My only option was to turn the fuchsias so only the one remaining side showed and to hope that no one got out of their cars to inspect the plants.

Fulfilling my duty for the day, I placed the Garden Club Tour sign in my yard and stationed myself at the entrance of our street, facing the oncoming traffic for directional assistance, my back squarely to the forest near our house. As time went by, my sweet husband came out of the front door, intent on bringing me a glass of iced tea. Suddenly, the glass went flying, his arms waved, and he yelled for all he was worth, "DON'T MOVE!"

As was often my response when being ordered to do something, I did exactly the opposite. I turned to face the woods where I spied what I believed to be the same fuchsia-munching moose from the night before. Yes, I remembered that more people die each year in Alaska by being trampled by a moose than from bear attacks, but this particular moose had gotten on my last nerve. In a fit of rage, I grabbed the Garden Club Tour welcome sign and took a mighty swing at the moose, who, faced with an incensed Garden Club "wannabee," took off in complete terror. Unfortunately, some of the arriving guests for the tour saw me swinging the sign in a rather menacing manner and took off as well.

That day became the stuff of urban legends in our little neighborhood but, alas, did not stand me in good stead with the Garden Club.

As I filled out my application for the Oxford Garden Club, I omitted the part about not growing my own fuchsias, the part about paying a ridiculously high price to have them wintered, and the part about having them half destroyed by the Bullwinkle of Brandilyn Drive. This left little for me to talk about, and I never did send in my application, somehow knowing that I wouldn't fit in. I did, however, take pride in the fact that though I couldn't grow anything to save my life, the Garden Club would be missing out on one determined moose wrangler.

Taking pride in accomplishments has become a way of life that has reach an epidemic level in society today. In watching the current human condition, I am often amazed at how important power and pride have become to people—not the power I joked about with the Garden Club but the power we think we can achieve through our own efforts, believing that our opinions are of greater importance than those of others, and seeing each hour as an opportunity to climb a little higher on the ladder of self-promotion. So many of us seem to strive for significance and power rather than contentment.

Being content with our place in life is a learned skill. We don't come into this world content but rather as a demanding baby who, for those early months, deftly and loudly exercises infantile power. A baby cries and we pick it up. A baby screams and we feed it. A baby fusses and we soothe it. As parents, it is up to us to teach our babies that loving and nurturing should become more important than having power and that selfishness should become selflessness. Hopefully, babies raised in a Christian home give up the power they once held, resting in contented relationships with parents, siblings, friends, and church families. Giving up power is hard; learning to be content is even harder. But Christ set the perfect example for us, coming to earth as a man when He could have come as the ultimate power broker.

Losing Max as unexpectedly as I did seemed to deprive me of my standing in the community and even how I saw myself. I "lost" friends we had enjoyed as couples. The invitations to functions dried up. I suddenly felt powerless in this new dynamic of my life. I somehow believed that being seen in the "right" groups and having the "right" friends were the relationships that gave me power and self-assurance. However, as the days and months progressed from the time of my husband's accident, I came to realize that, in truth, it was a personal, one-on-one relationship with Christ that brought power and strength to my life.

Earthly relationships, whether at work, at home, or in the community, often appear to bring a life of power and influence. In times of loss, when the dynamics of those relationships change or disappear altogether, sorrow is often the outcome of those changes.

Sorrow is that deep sadness that so many experience through loss, in part because our focus is on ourselves and those things we no longer have in our lives. Sorrow often blocks us from finding joy in the everyday things of God's creation.

In looking at the book of Job, we see a man who had lost everything that was important to him. He attempts to understand the calamities based on what he himself knows–on what his limited rational mind tells him. His focus is purely and completely on himself and his abilities. Indeed, in Chapters twenty-nine through thirty-one, Job uses the words "I," "my," or "me" one hundred twenty-nine times. Job, though a believer in God, has failed to put God at the forefront of his thoughts. However, in the midst of this self-centric mind-set, God began to speak and Job began to listen: "I know that you can do all things and that no purpose of yours can be thwarted" (Job 42:2).

When, through deep sorrow, we have shut out all our day-to-day norms, looking only inward and often spending days in isolation, there is amazingly a greater amount of time to spend in building a real relationship with the Lord. And that relationship brings the more powerful human condition of contentment. Prayer, the study of Scriptures, and relationships within the body of believers can bring about this power shift. For someone enduring a critical loss in their life, learning to be content in their current situation is a sign of healing from that loss, and that contentment comes from an ever-deepening relationship with Christ. "But godliness with contentment is a great gain for we brought nothing into this world and we cannot take anything out of this world" (1 Timothy 6:6).

I now want to be seen as a contented person who is not a slave to club memberships, social engagements or being part of the "right" group, and though there are now many more times in my life that seem sadly solitary, I know I am never truly alone. Jesus sought me day by day, taking the selfish "babe" that I was and transforming me into a child of God through the power of the Holy Spirit. I now yearn to be a reflection of the unearned love of Christ, who promised to bear burdens with me and lift me above my loss. I hope my God will allow me to be a gentle influence that might shine a light on someone else's darkened path, not because I am all-powerful, but because He was and is.

Reflections:

1. What are some of the things you've always desired or wanted to do in your life that have not come to pass? How do you feel about those omissions in your life?

2. Describe what a perfect day in your life would be?

3. Do you know others who appear to be content with their lives? Have you talked with them about their contentment? Read Ecclesiastes 3:11–13.

4. List three people in the Bible who appeared to be content. What was their relationship with God?

5. What steps can you take to be filled with greater contentment? Read Psalm 18:1–3

"Not that I am speaking of being in need, for I learned in whatever situation I am to be content."

Philippians 4:11

CHAPTER 8

" 'Tis the Gift to Be Simple "

"Simple Gifts," Early American Shaker Tune

"Every good gift and every perfect gift is from above,
coming down from the Father of lights."

James 1:17a

We just finished the summer birthday season here at the Miller home, and what a festive time it was! Treat started us off in Louisiana with my gift to him of Legos and a giant Nerf machine gun, which is now on little Max's Christmas list. It can shoot a hundred Nerf foam bullets in thirty seconds and is guaranteed to keep pesky sisters out of the boys' room. Gracie received a Calico Critters convertible filled with the "critters" and a boom box that came with the very necessary CD, *The Best of Abba*—what little girl doesn't need to know "Dancing Queen"? Shirley Cate got her first junior electric guitar to enhance her fascination with Elvis, and my son Patrick got some Tommy Bahama shirts to wear on his trip to Hawaii. Though I think he wanted a new weed eater, I held off giving Patrick any kind of tool, remembering the time we gave him a welding torch and he caught his hair on fire.

Then came my birthday. Shirley Cate gave me a decoration made out of Popsicle sticks, and I received the plants I had wanted for the front garden. I also received an embroidered pillow covered with the words to a beautiful hymn, a lovely scarf, an antique wooden bowl, and a great birthday cake with enough blue icing flowers to give everyone at the dinner table a blue tongue and a sugar high. It was natural that I thought about the love that went into the giving and receiving of gifts, knowing God has told us that it is "more blessed to give than to receive" (Acts 20:35).

As the first Christmas without the Captain approached, I pondered the gifts I had received over the past sixty-some years, and my mind got stuck on a Christmas memory that certainly showed my darker, corrupt side, and one I'd held in secret for many years. It was a frightful occasion that left my parents wondering if they had been given a changeling rather than their sweet middle daughter.

I was five. I had asked both Santa and God for a golden palomino horse, and the resulting chaos of this simple request led me to a life of petty crime just made for a personal injury lawyer.

Christmas 1955 was a pivotal moment in my gifting experience, young though I was. I still believed in Santa, definitely believed in God, and was, as any five-year-old would be, convinced that we should get exactly what we asked for. Thus, my request was for a golden palomino horse, a horse blanket, a saddle, a bridle, and a bale of hay–I was a thorough five-year-old. I asked for all this in a letter to Santa and in nightly prayers to God. I'd covered all my bases and looked forward to the time when Goldy (the horse's name I'd cleverly picked out) would be grazing in our postage stamp-sized backyard in our small residential neighborhood. I imagined her waiting to be ridden down the street, past the bus stop and fire hydrant, around the circle of friends' houses, and home again to my tiny backyard for more grazing.

Imagine the pain I felt when, on Christmas morning, I received a Davy Crockett guitar, a toy nurses' kit, and a majorette costume complete with a plumed hat, baton, and tasseled white boots. My older sister got a Madame Alexander doll, an Easy-Bake Oven, and a biology set that included a microscope, some real "slice your finger open" glass slides, and honest-to-goodness dissecting needles.

One can never know the betrayal I felt with no saddle or hay bale in sight, and to make matters worse, my sister proceeded to ridicule me for thinking I was getting that horse. Now I could say, like Judas Iscariot, Satan entered the heart of a disappointed five-year-old that day, but my mother would tell you it was just pure meanness on my part. Whatever the reason, I picked up one of those new dissecting needles and gave my sister's arm the **tiniest** of little pokes. And though my intent was to make her be quiet, she howled and went to tattle on me.

I am not normally violent, but sibling harassment had pushed me to my limit. It really was just a *teeny tiny poke* and probably wouldn't even have left much of a mark, though it did draw a single drop of blood. I readied myself for my mother to get out the board, an instrument of discipline feared by everyone in the household, including the cat. But I lucked out that day. My sister returned pouting because the swat with the board wasn't coming. My mother was in the hospital having a baby, and Grandma B wasn't up for using corporal punishment. I remember pondering how my request for a horse had gotten mixed up with a new sister.

Ever the inventive five-year-old, I suggested to my pouty sister that we might as well put her blood to good use, so we smeared it onto one of the glass slides and looked at it under the microscope. I thought the blood looked cool; my sister promptly threw up all over the presents still under the tree. I didn't get a swat that day, but I was sent to the corner as punishment for making my sister sick.

I've learned a lot about gift-giving over the years, starting with a sermon I once heard when the preacher told the male members of the congregation *not* to give their wives vacuum cleaners for Christmas. "Too practical," he said. I'm happy to report that not one of my four vacuum cleaners came from my husband. I could, however, always tell which gifts were from the Captain; they were the ones with the twenty stick-on bows, often sporting the wrong season of paper.

Though Max gave the best and most thoughtful gifts as we got older, he had some missteps early on in our marriage. There was the year I wanted new bedroom slippers for Christmas, and instead, he got me a Dazey Donut Factory so he could have fresh donuts every morning. Being the culinary giant that I am, I made them for him once, and he never asked for them again. I remember the year Grandma Shanahan gave Daddy a jar filled with all of his old baby teeth, though I think he wanted a drill. Daddy gave Mom a hatchet one year for Mother's Day in case she ever wanted to go camping . . . she didn't. And I happily remember the year we were all at church on Christmas Eve when the rumor was circulating that our friend, John, had gotten his wife, Ann, a mink coat. We discovered on Christmas morning that the rumor mill must have been hard of hearing since what John had actually gotten Ann was not a mink coat, but a baby goat named Baaaah-bette. Such are the tales of gift giving and gift disappointment.

My mother never used the hatchet, my dad bought his own drill, the donut maker went into the garage sale, and the Easy-Bake Oven made the worst biscuits ever. But every year, as I decide what gifts to give, I truly hope my grandchildren never ask for a horse, as I, like my parents, will be reduced to Easy-Bake Ovens and majorette costumes. Alas, the Davy Crockett guitar is no longer in production.

As I ponder this seasonal dilemma, I recall two lessons I've learned over the years: some of the most precious gifts are made out of Popsicle sticks, and the giving of gifts can be much more fun than the receiving. Watching the surprise and joy in the eyes of the recipient is a gift in and of itself. And I am filled with the thought that though God intended us to be givers and not just receivers, *He* wanted to be the ultimate gift giver, with mankind as the ultimate recipient.

I was thinking of past gifts, given and received, when I got some Christmas gift tags in the mail from one of the charities I support. It was a bit early to be thinking of Christmas, so I filed them away for later use. The word *From* on those labels stuck in my mind and I thought about the gifts I had received from people *and* God, the greatest one being His Son born on Christmas Day.

God has always been the ultimate gift giver, and if one thinks my request for a horse was an impractical gift, consider the gift of a tiny baby sent to bring salvation to a fallen world. God wisely knew that for us to accept Jesus as our Savior, we would need someone to whom we could relate: a child growing up as we had, being tempted as we are, suffering the sorrow of a loss, and grieving as we have. Ray Stedman, in his book *Talking with the Father*, made the point that God wanted to give us the gifts of power and strength, but we had to be willing to receive those gifts.[4] Being open to gifts is one of those gates we need in our protective wall through which Christ can enter our lives, working through the Holy Spirit, to lift our hearts from the grieving over losses to the grateful receipt of His freely offered gifts. And, once given those gifts, we are urged to use them so that others might receive them as well. Gifts such as grace, kindness, peace, faithfulness love, joy–these trump any package we could ever give or receive.

I suspect that my parents wanted to give me a horse when I was five because they loved me and wanted me to be happy. However, they were also wise enough to know that such a gift would be full of problems and not necessarily provide me with the proof of their love that a five-year-old envisioned.

God, who has loved us like a parent and, who can adopt us into His family, knew that we needed that impractical gift of a baby born on Christmas far more than anything else we could ever want. God gave us the gift of a Savior! And through the grace of that Savior, I am surrounded by friends, family, and a church, giving me the gift of a life filled with some joys and some losses but complete with a Dazey Donut Factory and Popsicle sticks. My hope is that there are Popsicle sticks and a loving Savior in your future as well.

Reflections:

1. What is your favorite gift you have ever received from someone? Your least favorite?

2. Did your feelings about that gift ever change over the course of time?

3. What has been the most important gift and the most important giver in your life? Can the two be separated? Read John 6:33–35.

4. Would you rather give or receive a gift?

5. What gifts has God given you? Have you ever wanted to *return them*? Read 1Corinthians 1:7–8.

"For by grace you have been saved through faith. And this is not your own doing; it is the gift of God."

Ephesians 2:8

CHAPTER 9

"A Little Bit of Chicken Fried"

From "Chicken Fried," The Zack Brown Band

---

*"Yet he did not leave himself without witness, for he did
good by giving you rains from heaven and fruitful seasons,
satisfying your hearts with food and gladness."*

Acts 14:17

We had our church community group here at my house last month,
and one of the best things we do as a group is eat. Certainly, we enjoy one
another's company as we hold each person up in prayer, but we eat really,
really well while doing it!

With so many good cooks coming to my home, I am constantly
reminded of what a bad cook I am, not to mention what a picky eater I
am as well. Some thoughtful member of our group always brings vegetables, one of those basic food groups that I am convinced we could do
without. My community group friends have tried to persuade me that my
eating habits are somewhat lacking. I've heard such remedies for my dislike
of broccoli as "cover it with cheese and you'll never taste the broccoli" or
"put catsup on it and it tastes like shrimp"—I hate shrimp! I also gag over

Brussels sprouts, onions, tomatoes, cucumbers, spinach, kale, cabbage, asparagus, and peas. I've probably left out some of my "dislikes" but, suffice it to say, the only green things that enter my mouth are iceberg lettuce, avocados, green olives, green apples, and pistachio ice cream. For fifty-three years Max put up with my foodie idiosyncrasies, and it's a good thing he knew how to cook so that he didn't die of scurvy, or rickets, or whatever it is you get from the lack of leafy green vegetables.

One night, while chatting with our community group, I related the horror story of going to dinner at the home of some Korean friends we had met through the Naval Postgraduate School in Monterey, California. They had wanted to thank us for sponsoring them within the school community, and the wife had worked extremely hard on a traditional Korean dinner. There were any number of unknown delicacies, many with a tinge of green, which precluded them from entering my mouth. My sense of the gourmet focused on a single menu item that I had recognized: sliced apples.

Our host family noticed the rather limited menu items on my plate, and I could see that the Captain was worried about the start of an international incident. That must have been why he put a healthy scoop of what he told me was rotini—macaroni curls—onto my plate, balancing off the one-sided fruit extravaganza. Thankful to him for finding something that wouldn't make me gag, I loaded my fork with as many noodles as it could carry and placed the fork into my mouth, prepared to have that "this is so yummy, and thank you for the delicious meal" look on my face. It is a credit to my years of having to take one bite of everything on my plate while growing up that I didn't choke, gag, or run for the bathroom as the "noodles" slithered down my throat. My eyes watered and my stomach lurched all while maintaining that prepared look of gratitude for my hosts. As I was reaching for the large glass of tea, which thankfully was nearby, I saw Max's grin out of the corner of my watering eye. I also saw the grins of both our sons and knew immediately that my family of "guys" had put one over on Mom once again. Our hostess looked at me with such delight and remarked that she had never seen anyone eat such a healthy portion of pickled baby octopus tentacles. My vow for revenge was immediate. The Captain would pay, and it wouldn't be from eating my cooking . . . though that would have been sufficiently painful.

Revenge, when it came a full ten years after the octopus incident, was a serendipitous event, and I was finally successful in my payback plot. It involved the many guidebooks I had read about Alaska, the state in which we were then living; those guidebooks told the reader everything they needed to know about the "Last Frontier," including many of the delicacies enjoyed by its indigenous people.

The "great payback" occurred on an evening when a Japanese battle-ship came to the port of Anchorage, a momentous occasion because this was the first Japanese naval vessel to visit Alaska since the end of World War II. The event was marked with streamers and banners, speeches, and lots of uniformed officers. Military bands played and food was in abundance. Out of respect for my husband's position as Captain of the Port, the Japanese Command assigned a naval ensign to see to our every need, including making sure our plates were amply supplied and our saké boxes were full. Max left to use the bathroom—"the head" on a ship—when our ensign arrived with a new offering from the buffet table. It looked just like "chicken on a stick", a culinary staple at home in Oxford, Mississippi, with those bits of chicken breast that are battered, deep-fried, and served on a wooden skewer. Since I could not imagine that the Japanese Navy would be serving such a traditionally American fare, I asked about it before accepting the proffered skewer. Our ensign replied that it was "muktuk".

My revenge-filled mind dredged up the translation of "muktuk" from one of my cherished guidebooks and that knowledge provided me with the perfect information needed to exact my revenge. The Captain returned from the bathroom, and I presented him with a skewer of deep-fried morsels of meat. He asked, with homesick wistfulness, "Is this chicken on a stick?" I didn't exactly say yes but only smiled with my "this looks so yummy" countenance perfected ten years earlier. He took a big healthy bite

71

and, unlike me who had held myself together with a mouth full of pickled baby octopus tentacles, he gagged and ran for the nearest trash can, spitting out the deep-fried *whale blubber* that had once looked so appealing. The ensign was aghast at the Captain's behavior, but I saved face by telling the ensign, "He never could hold his whale blubber." I seem to remember leaving shortly thereafter and driving through Kentucky Fried Chicken on the way home.

Now that Max is gone, I rarely fix myself a real meal. Grazing has become the new normal for me. I keep lots of frozen meals on hand, several jars of peanut butter, and plenty of popcorn. When I buy truly unhealthy foods at the grocery store (see Chapter 3 for discussion on Hostess CupCakes and donuts), I rationalize that they are for the Grands. But then, when I take pleasure in sharing my newly bought snacks with the children, I understand that it's often the company with whom I am eating in addition to the quality of the food that makes the meal delightful and joyous. I have, however, found some contentment in eating alone because I know I'll be saved from raw baby octopus tentacles and deep-fried whale blubber. Bring on the Hostess CupCakes!

When your life suffers the loss of a loved one, the loss of a job or the loss of a way of life, something as simple as eating a meal, whether because of that special dish you had previously shared, that special place you always went to for lunch, or that recipe you traded with a now distant friend, becomes a memory that often brings a profound sense of loneliness. When I first lost Max, in an effort to recreate the "married meals," I made a point of setting the table for whatever meal I was eating; I used my good dishes and a glass goblet rather than the old plastic cups stuffed in a bottom drawer. Occasionally, I went out to eat by myself, but that did nothing to lift my spirits. What did lift my spirits was the eating of the "spiritual food" talked about in the Bible.

The Bible talks about food from the very beginning, when Adam and Eve were told what they could and could not eat in the garden of Eden. At that point, God was certainly providing for their physical well-being by offering all the delicacies He had created, with one small exception: fruit from the Tree of the Knowledge of Good and Evil. In telling them what NOT to eat, God presented them with the consequences of discovering evil and ultimately death, but their hunger for the things not of God led to the downfall of mankind.

As the scriptures progress to the time of the Messiah, we see the image of food and the satiation of hunger used as a metaphor for one of the greatest of God's provisions. The apostle John explains, "For the bread of God is he who comes down from heaven and gives life to the world" (John 6:33). Indeed, Jesus declares, "I am the bread of life; whoever comes to me shall not hunger and whoever believes in me shall not thirst" (John 6:35).

Christ understood that while physical hunger can kill the body, spiritual hunger can kill both the body and the soul. To sustain us through loss, Christ has offered us a spiritual food that fills one with hope rather than despair, and that hope directs one to a life everlasting. He has done this by asking us to partake of the bread at Holy Communion as a reminder of His life sacrificed for our sins (Luke 22: 19–20). He has done this by teaching us to pray for our daily bread (Matthew 6: 9–13). He has taught us that spiritual food is more filling and long lasting than earthly food and drink (John 4:13–14). When we focus on Christ as the means of satisfying our hunger, we will eventually leave the sorrow of our loss behind and begin to "hunger and thirst after righteousness" so that we "shall be satisfied" (Matthew 5:6).

Reflections:

1. Read John 4: 7–14. What kind of water was Jesus talking about so that the Samaritan woman at the well might be satisfied?

2. Read Luke 22:7–20. Why do you think Jesus instituted communion? How do you feel as you take communion?

3. When you snack all day, are you fully satisfied at night? Do you get more fulfillment when you read entire passages of scripture or just brief memory verses?

4. List some ways God has provided physical food in order to fill His people with a spiritual meal. Read Genesis 2:8–9, Exodus 16:3–4, 13, 35. Mark 8:1–8, John 2:9–10, and Psalm 36:7–9.

"For he satisfies the longing soul, and the hungry soul he fills with good things"

Psalm 107:9

CHAPTER 10

When Good Things Happen to Bad People

"For God has consigned all to disobedience so that he may have mercy on all."

Romans 11:32

My grandson, Treat, has renamed his father Mr. Safety Hazzard, a perfect moniker for Patrick. After listening to the stories my sons have told at our family meals since Max died, it would be an understatement to say that, for us as parents, ignorance was bliss. I have come to believe that the newly added eighth wonder of the world is that my sons survived to adulthood.

Patrick's name change came about on his son's eighth birthday, when I had gotten Treat a contraption to attach to his swing set so that the "swinger" simulates riding a surfboard or a skateboard. I know that sounds dangerous, but it was on the parents' official list of approved gifts. After Patrick and Treat's last *real* skateboard experience, which included a broken collarbone, a broken elbow, and a broken tooth, all suffered by the **parent** in charge, my daughter-in-law, Rachel, wisely outlawed the skateboards, and I guess they thought this gift might be a fun alternative; it did not specifically require a safety helmet, so it just had to be safer.

Treat, excited to start "surfing and skating," got a jackknife to open the box. As Treat was brandishing the knife toward the closed box, Patrick jumped in. "Give me the knife. You'll cut your finger off." It reminded me of one of the scenes from a favorite holiday movie in which Ralphie wants a BB gun, but his parents keep saying, "No! You'll shoot your eye out." We should have listened!

Patrick, again the adult in this scene, snatched the knife from Treat's hand, whereupon he promptly cut himself. It was a deep cut and bled profusely all over the gift box and the kitchen floor but, thankfully, missed the birthday cake. Rachel called for a trip to the emergency room and for stitches while Patrick hid the car keys and *strongly* suggested that wouldn't be happening. I drove to Walgreens for bandages and antibacterial ointment. By the time I returned, Rachel had found the car keys, but the patient had barricaded himself in his office. It was at that point that Treat dubbed his father Mr. Safety Hazzard. I doubt seriously that Treat, at eight years of age, understood the definition of an oxymoron, but his teacher would have been proud he had used one correctly.

What is it about children, boys in particular, that leads to calamity and chaos, all in the name of good, clean fun? Suffice it to say, with greater technology and the mechanical ways in which good clean fun can now manifest itself, I'm surprised there haven't been more people dubbed Mr. Safety Hazzard. For example, did you know that children have discovered that if they work in pairs, they can use the garage door like a ride at Disneyland–one to manipulate the garage door button and ask that all arms and legs remain safely inside the vehicle until it comes to a complete stop and the other child who is just along for the ride? I have heard rumors that garage door companies are now putting weight limits on their products.

Listening to stories such as these as they are told and retold at family get-togethers and as the next generation of small impressionable children are within hearing–and if they can write, taking notes–I am filled with alarm and a great degree of guilt that I didn't know about many of these incidents. Were we bad parents, or were our boys just mentally gifted when it came to mischief? Here are some examples of some of the stories that have come to light over the last few years. I pray that the Captain didn't know about them either. As the remaining parent, it would make me feel ever so much better!

Patrick: Exhibit A

I recall the time we lost power to the house, and all the circuit breakers tripped at the same time. Our inventive oldest son likened himself to a young Thomas Edison as he tried to rewire his little brother's electric record player so it would run backward, thereby allowing him to listen to the mythical bad words on Michael Jackson's *Thriller*. It didn't work, but it did lead Patrick in a direction other than electrical engineering as a career path.

Patrick: Exhibit B

One day, Patrick, age ten, came home from visiting his friend Mac and headed straight to his room, without supper or playing records backward. Patrick and Mac had been practicing their riflery skills with an *unauthorized* BB gun when they shot a frog. The frog died, but, according to Patrick, it was not before it stared directly at Patrick with its one remaining little froggy eye, letting him know that the senseless killing God's creatures was wrong, unless, of course, it's a snake! The nightmares continued for a week before the story of the Great Frog Murder was told truthfully, to say nothing of the unauthorized BB gun.

Patrick: Exhibit C

Our original family cat detested Patrick and somehow passed Patrick's reputation along to subsequent family cats until they all despised him; cats, like elephants, never forget. This feline animosity came about when Patrick was reminiscing about his childhood dream of becoming an astronaut. He lashed ten helium balloons to the cat to see if she could fly. She couldn't. And following NASA's protocol about not contaminating space with germs from Earth, he vacuumed her.

Ryan: Exhibit A

Ryan, having a mischievous streak like his older brother, was suddenly no longer invited to the Davis' house for play dates with his friend, Jeff. Apparently, Ryan had made a cassette tape and exchanged it for the official one that came with Jeff's Teddy Ruxpin talking bear. Instead of asking if Jeff would like to be his friend, Teddy suddenly blared out a song by Metallica, KISS, or one of those groups that have scary painted faces and scream things about eating bats and handling snakes. I suspect Jeff's nightmares lasted a week too.

Ryan Exhibit B

One Saturday morning, with nothing better to do, Ryan tied his battery-powered Tonka truck to one of my husband's fishing poles. He placed the truck in the upstairs floor heating vent to see if it could circumnavigate our house. The plan was for the fishing pole to be used to reel the truck back in case the expedition had to be aborted. Magellan failed. The fishing pole got lodged in the heating vent, and the truck, which was stuck in the middle of the living room ceiling by that time, continued to make a very loud *vrooom vrooom* for many days to come.

Tiring of the truck fiasco, the boys collected every shiny-surfaced object they could find, taking them downstairs to the family room to see how many times they could bounce the remote signal from one shiny surface to another to turn the TV on and off. This, unlike the truck expedition, was very successful.

Admittedly, I was home for these events but busy fixing the washing machine, whose timing cycle had frozen again. Using my ball-peen hammer, as I had successfully done in the past, I tried to find just the right spot to give the machine a few good whacks and jar the cycle switch loose. That day, however, the sweet spot on the washing machine was a bit more elusive, and my ball-peen strikes were a bit louder and more frequent than in the past. There may have been some yelling aimed at the washing machine as well.

That must have been the reason we didn't hear the Captain come through the front door at nine o'clock in the morning after a long night of working in his Coast Guard capacity to get a grounded ship seaworthy again. Upon hearing the *vrooom vrooom* of the Tonka truck in the middle of the living room ceiling, seeing the fishing pole half eaten by the floor vent, hearing the repeated on/off of the TV, and the frantic strikes of a ball-peen hammer, he walked right back out the door. I never did find out where he went. Maybe he went for donuts. I don't think they sold beer early.

I suppose my parents did a better job of convincing me that they would *always* find out what I'd been up to. As a result, I was one of those ultra-good girls throughout high school and college. No drinking, no smoking, and no boys in my dorm room. I even turned down tickets to see the rock musical, *Hair*, I *just knew* my mother , *nine hours away*, would somehow find out I'd gone.

Our boys never bought the claim that we had eyes in the backs of our heads, though Ryan occasionally would lift my hair just to make sure. Neither did they believe that we had a vast network of spies checking on their every move. Despite all the ingenious pranks, failed adventures and "boys will be boys" moments, they have become wonderful men, in great part due to the example set by their father. Children can be inventive, mischievous, and even secretive at times, but we parents are called to guide them, nurture them, hold them accountable, and, above all, love them as our Father in heaven loves us, His wayward children.

Adam and Eve sinned, and they felt guilty. They hid from God, and when He asked what they had done, they blamed God, each other, and the serpent. This sounds just like our children. The difference is that, as a parent, I can't see everything; God most assuredly does. And like Max and I had to sometimes do with our boys, God punished Adam and Eve, not because He didn't love them, but because *He did*. Proverbs 3:11 says, "My son, do not despise the LORD'S discipline or be weary of his reproof, for the LORD reproves him whom he loves as a father the son in whom he delights."

I was speaking with a committed Christian lady who had recently lost her husband and I was telling her about my belief that God loves us like a father does his child. When I talked with her about her loss, she told me that she felt like she was being punished by God. I certainly understood her feelings but hearing her say it saddened me greatly and made me wonder if she subscribed to the long-held belief that if there is sorrow or sickness or calamity in one's life, it must be because God was punishing them for their sins. In John 9:2, this idea was posed to Jesus: "And his disciples asked him, 'Rabbi, who sinned, this man or his parents, that he was born blind.'" Jesus answered that the man was not blind due to sin but so that when Jesus restored the man's sight, God's works might be displayed through him. The reasons for God's purposes in our lives are like the blind man, not for punishment but for illumination.

The simple truth is that bad things happen to good people and good things happen to bad people. That is the way of this world because sin entered the garden of Eden. But any kind of great loss can set in motion a long-range "good" that we may never see in our lifetimes. Romans 8:28 says, "And for those who love God, all things work together for good, for those who are called according to his purpose."

If my children had never done anything wrong, I would never have had the opportunity to teach them right from wrong or demonstrate my deep love and desire to offer them grace and forgiveness. If God punished someone because they were a sinner, that would mean **we would all** suffer terrible tragedies and calamities because **we are all sinners**: "for all have sinned and fall short of the glory of God" (Romans 3:23). We can take comfort from the fact that Christ went to die on the Cross so that punishment for sin would be taken on Himself and we, who were not deserving to be spared, would be. It is through the bad things that happen that we are given a glimpse of God's ultimate mercy, forgiveness and glory.

I don't know what good has specifically come from Max's death that might affect many. He was just one man in a small southern town, but I do know that my faith in a sovereign and loving God is deeper now than before the accident. I do know that the boy whose car hit Max got a scholarship and went on to attend a teaching college. I do know that people joined our church after attending Max's memorial service because of the gospel message proclaimed there. These things may not be the ultimate purpose of his death, but they are part of the outcome. We *must* look for the good. We know it is there because we have a God who is totally good, merciful, and insightful as to our future needs and the lessons we should learn.

Reflections

1. Do you know someone who seems to have gotten ahead/succeeded in life by cheating or lying? Did their actions tempt you to behave the same way? If not, why not? Read Titus 3:3–8.

2. Do you know someone who considered themselves to be unlucky in life? Do they blame someone other than themselves? Do they blame God? Make a list comparing their trials to those of Job. Read Job 33:29–31 and 42:2.

3. Have you ever compared your misfortunes to those of others and ask, "why me?" Have you ever considered your misfortunes as punishment? Read Romans 5:1–5.

4. In the midst of trials in your life, do you still believe that God has blessed you? If so, in what ways? Read Ephesians 1:7–10 and 2 Corinthians 5:21.

"Beloved, do not be surprised at the fiery trial when it comes upon you to test you, as though something strange were happening to you. But rejoice insofar as you share Christ's sufferings, that you may also rejoice and be glad when his glory is revealed."

1 Peter 4:12–13

CHAPTER 11

"And They Called It Puppy Love"

"Puppy Love," Paul Anka

"But God showed his love for us that while we were still sinners, Christ died for us."

Romans 5:8

Since my husband died, there have been some additions to our family. Both of our sons got dogs, and these pets have certainly made for some interesting events and conversations.

Patrick acquired a black Cocker spaniel puppy to live with his other Cockers, Spike and Buffy. The children promptly named him Buster Dude Miller. They had their Cappy in mind with the name Buster, as Max had always said that "Buster" would be his choice if we ever got a dog. I've thought about getting a dog myself, and I guess I would name him Buster II, but the cat has launched a protest, so I remain dogless.

Though I have been referred to by my sons and the Grands as the "cat lady," I have long believed that dogs express their love and devotion for their humans so much more than cats do. Cats greet you at the door with "You're late. My dinner bowl is only partially filled. What do you mean staying out 'til all hours? I was forced to amuse myself by knocking over your glass of iced tea and playing Wheel of Fortune with the toilet paper roll." Dogs, on the other hand, seem genuinely delighted to see you. They remind me of how Max made me feel when I would arrive home from a trip. I think if my husband had been a dog, he'd have been a Basset Hound—slow and steady with an unabashed enjoyment of taking naps on the couch. I'd have named him Speedy.

Buster Dude Miller, however, is anything but slow and steady. Indeed, he rarely sits calmly, loves to eat the couch rather than nap on it, and is terrified that the doggie door will hit him in the backside as he goes through; therefore, *he doesn't* go through, leading to many statements such as "Bad dog!" and "*Not* on the antique rug!"

Being the dog lover that Patrick is (or being the dad who caved to the puppy eyes of my eleven-year-old granddaughter), Buster is about to get a golden retriever puppy buddy. The saving grace of this canine acquisition is that it will probably require a larger doggie door with a longer close time, encouraging Buster to at least make it to the deck, if not the yard.

Though my son, Ryan, has not seen fit to install a doggie door (possibly because little Max would use it as an escape hatch), he did see fit to get a dog. Harry is a Golden-doodle that an apartment-dwelling friend was giving away. Harry is large, affable, and given to eating stray socks, which then requires a healthy dose of hydrogen peroxide to expel said sock. The children have taken to wearing no socks at all–it's safer for all that way. Harry would make a great watchdog, not for his ferocity but for his ability to knock down the assailant and beat him to death with his tail, which is a case study of perpetual motion.

Once outside, Harry's entire body is constantly moving, running with joyful abandon through a sock-free zone. He discovered the lake and squirrels simultaneously one day when he jumped for and caught a squirrel while performing his version of a jackknife with a double twist off the high dive into the lake. I awarded him a ten for effort, but his ripple upon entering the water was too large, so I gave him a minus eight for technique. The squirrel managed to escape when Harry hit the water. And the *crowd went wild*—truly an Olympic-quality event.

With Olympic style maneuvers not limited to dogs, some family pets show amazing athletic skills. Who could forget the record-breaking run of Pickles, our neighbors' pot-bellied pig? Pickles had long been the free-range pig of the neighborhood, snuffling along, eating the birdseed from under my bird feeder, or standing still long enough to deposit pig nuggets, which the Captain hated hitting with the lawnmower. We all endured Pickles because we dearly loved our neighbors.

The track and field event with Pickles unfolded when our son, Ryan, was asked to "pigsit" while the neighbors were away. Saying that Pickles was overlarge for a pot-bellied pig would be an understatement. Her dietary downfall was dog food, especially dog biscuits. She waddled slowly on her little pig feet, doing an amazing job of supporting a girth that was at least three times the normal size of her fellow pet, Milk Dud, the dog. Her owners encouraged Pickles to eat normal pig food–whatever that may be–but Milk Dud's dog dish stayed suspiciously empty.

Author and illustrator Charles Schulz would have had his canine character, Snoopy, on the top of his doghouse, typewriter perched precariously on the roof, writing, "It was a dark and stormy night . . ." But it wasn't. It was the hottest day of the century, possibly the millennium, and Ryan was pig-sitting when a motorcycle came up the street and backfired while Pickles was free-ranging. Weight and little pig's feet notwithstanding, Pickles flew down the street at record speed, and while she didn't leap over hedges, she did leave perfect pot-belly shaped holes in her wake. Ryan screamed, "Bring the dog biscuits!" and took off after the racing side of bacon.

Pickles almost made it to the end of the street before Ryan caught up with her. Her head was buried deep in a bush, obviously under the assumption that if she couldn't see, she couldn't be seen. Max, Ryan's new wife, Erin, and I arrived with the emergency ration of dog biscuits and watched as Ryan tried to coax Pickles back up the street. She didn't like being prodded, she didn't like walking over the driveways she had only moments before traversed, and she was overheating. She would stagger a few steps and then refuse to budge; we were beginning to overheat as well. To hurry this porcine parade along, I ran home and filled my large watering can. Other neighbors flew into action, providing us with a huge golf umbrella and coming up with two sheets of plywood that our neighborhood 4-H student assured us would act like a pig chute and force Pickles to move forward in a straight line. And thus, we progressed: I watered Pickles, Erin shaded her with the umbrella, Max and the neighbor manned the pig chute, and Ryan continued to walk backwards holding the bribe of dog biscuits in front of Pickles' snout. The procession took forty-five minutes to travel through four front yards and across four driveways which originally had been a five second run, leading to not only a heat-prostrated pig but sunburned pig-herders. Pickles finally collapsed on her overlarge pig bed under her overlarge pig fan. Milk Dud got his dog biscuits back, and the neighborhood went to our back fridge for some well-deserved cold beers.

It was a week later when we learned that the 4-H student had written a short story for his fourth-grade class in which he described the old pig herder and his elderly wife (I think that was me and Max) and their able-bodied sidekicks. While the teacher didn't believe a word of the story, the child did get an A+. You can't make this stuff up. Or as Greg Gutfeld on Fox News would say, "Animals are great, animals are great."

When I suffered my loss, my silly, annoying cat was a great comfort to me, and I began to think about pets in heaven. I wish I could know about pets in heaven, but the Bible does not indicate that Fluffy, Cuddles, Duke, or even Pickles will be with us when we come before God. Maybe there will be pets when, someday, we enjoy heaven on earth. But for now, I am thankful that our pets give us a tiny glimpse of that pure, unearned, unconditional love that God has for us, providing our earthly time with moments of true devotion. Even our junkyard cat, Punkin, grieved for Max, waiting patiently by the back door each day for my husband to come home from work at the normal time.

Our pets give us a glimpse of how to live outside ourselves when it comes to loss. Their focus is generally not on themselves but their masters. And so too should our focus during loss be on our Master, not on ourselves.

When loss fills us with grief, a focus on God rather than ourselves keeps us grounded in a way nothing else can. When we are tempted to sin, realigning our sights on the goodness and redemption offered by Christ's atoning blood can change our penchant for sin into a desire to please the Master, turning sorrow, self-absorption, and loss into a desire for service and praise. And in that effort to serve and praise Him, we are rewarded with some healing of the grief-stricken spirit.

Unfortunately, focusing on the Master and seeking to please Him are not always the actions of others. In our "me-first" society, where having a Heavenly Master is considered stifling and where something that curbs the all-consuming personal wants and desires of this world is deemed cruelly judgmental, we are pressured to take part in an unrepentant society. Many people around us, including friends and family, lead lives that are antithetical to the gospel of Christ and it is in these relationships that we must be strong in our convictions of loving one another but without forgetting our obedience to our Master.

Blessedly, we have an example in Christ who, though He lived in this world was not of this world. Even knowing that not everyone would readily accept His offered redemption, "Christ died for the ungodly" (Romans 5:6). He went to the Cross for us, and though He came to us as a man and lived within this sin-filled world, He never succumbed to the ways of this world; His ear was always tuned to His Master's voice.

Reflections:

1. How does God show unconditional love in your life? Can you still sense His love when enduring a loss? Read Lamentations 3:22–33.

2. List some places in the Bible where God's unconditional love was shown.

3. Have you ever lost a friend or family member because of your Christian beliefs? Did you feel a sense of anger or loss? Did you just accept the loss? Did you seek to share the gospel of Christ?

4. Read Luke 6:40. What steps are you taking in your life where you are actively allowing the Master to train you?

"For the moment, all discipline seems painful rather than pleasant, but later it yields the peaceful fruit of righteousness to those who have been trained by it."

Hebrews 12:1

CHAPTER 12

Don't Ever Get Old, Jami, Don't Ever Get Old

Quote from Stephen Timothy Shanahan

"LORD, you have searched me and known me! You know when I sit down and when I rise up; you discern my thoughts from afar. . . . Your eyes saw my unformed substance; in your book were written, every one of them; the days that were formed for me, when as yet there were none of them."

Psalm 139:1–2, 16

Since my husband's accident and in less than three years, I had four surgeries. I admit to being a little irritated that the Captain was not here to hold my hand, be my cheerleader, and, of course, cook for me. It never dawned on me how much Max took care of me when I was down and out until he wasn't here to be my advocate. For that, I forgive him—well, maybe not the cooking part, but everything else. I suspect what irritates me is that while he's resting in the loving arms of the Father, I'm down here getting old. My plan was never to get old, let alone have so many health problems. I suddenly feel like a grandparent instead of the fun lady who lives next door to her grandchildren. But, like it or not, here I am, white-haired and covered with new surgical scars.

My aging has suddenly forced me to relate better to those people around me to whom I've always felt a bit superior because I *couldn't possibly be as old as they were.* However, as my time as a grandparent continues to lengthen, I find myself looking at these people with a new awareness and (I can't believe I'm saying this) a sense of kinship.

To that point, I was in Walmart the other day and noticed a woman who appeared to be about my age standing alongside me in the craft aisle. In her cart was a baby carrier/car seat contraption. I was behind her cart, so all I could see was the woman's face and the back of the contraption. What struck me was the look of complete adoration she was raining down on the unseen baby. She leaned in and made silly noises at the child, and then laughed in delight as her noises seemed to bring a joyful response. She asked the baby if he/she wanted his/her binky, at which point she whipped out a pacifier from her pocket and proffered it into the car seat. She asked the baby if he/she wanted his/her bottle, and the bottle magically appeared. She was having such fun!

I, on the other hand, was buying paint remover to eliminate the orange paint little Max had spilled on my light beige carpet when he decided to see what paint tasted like. Not able to resist joining the Happy Grandmother Club, I asked if it was a boy or girl (it was a girl) and if this was her first grandchild. She responded positively and confessed that she had no idea how much fun being a grandparent would be. I admitted she was right, chose the paint remover I hoped would work on the color orange, and headed to check out. As I was leaving the check-out lane, she came out of the adjacent lane, and I could finally see what the little darling looked like.

I was suddenly transported back to my former church in Long Beach, Mississippi, where a Cabbage Patch doll with the name Ricky Tyronne had portrayed Baby Jesus in the children's Christmas program for four years running. This lady's granddaughter may not have had the first name of Ricky Tyronne, but her last name was definitely Cabbage Patch. Yes, this grandmother was buying Pampers for and feeding a bottle to a Cabbage Patch doll—a doll whose fabric face was horribly stained from previous feedings and appeared to be missing one eye.

I watched in amazement as this woman gave me a "welcome to the Grandmother Club" wave and headed toward the exit, all the while whispering to the sleeping "baby." My first instinct was to laugh out loud, and I admit to a few chuckles escaping my mouth. But then I was overcome with sadness because this woman had to make do with a doll, whereas I had a living breathing grandson who, though he tried to drink my craft paint, could also knock on my front door at six-thirty in the morning to tell me he had come for peanut butter toast. And the thought that left me speechless and with fewer chuckles was that as I got older, I might become befuddled, feeble-minded, and given to buying Cabbage Patch dolls off the internet. This lady was perfectly content and had no inkling that her behavior was a little suspect.

I, on the other hand, began to worry about my life ahead. To further add to my concern about the aging process, I stepped in a hole the next week, broke my foot in two places, and tore up my knee.

Going through the broken foot and the two knee surgeries by myself was so very hard. I was afraid, feeling helpless, and, worst of all, I was not allowed to go home after the final knee replacement because no one was there to care for me. Instead, I went to live in a nursing home for thirty days. There I could get all the physical and occupational therapy I needed and, hopefully, return to my normal grandmotherly life.

I lovingly took to calling my new and temporary home the "Institution," and while the staff was very kind and the therapy was great, I got a first-hand look at what it meant to truly get old. I passed my days between scheduled therapy sessions by reading mysteries, doing crosswords, watching TV, and playing the occasional game of Uno when Ryan brought the Grands to visit. I had my son bring me my piano music so I could hobble down the hall to the big dining room where they had a piano, but I was run out of there by an irate group of seniors waiting for the next bingo game, which wasn't slated to start until some two hours later. I once sat in a narrow hall for two hours with all my fellow Institution residents while we waited for a tornado warning to be lifted, with the main topic of discussion being whether or not the bingo game would have to be postponed. I got helped to the shower every other day at five o'clock in the morning. I learned to rely on the bacon biscuit each morning for breakfast but to NEVER order the scrambled eggs. And I watched each day as the dining room staff tried to encourage a lady to eat; she responded only when she was allowed to hold "her baby," which, of course, was a Cabbage Patch doll.

My days rolled along, filled with boredom but also with great physical improvement. Toward the end of my stay at the Institution, a new nurse came in to check on me. She was far older than the other nurses, but this was explained when she told me she was the nursing supervisor. She inspected my room and made marks and notes on her clipboard. I had a machine that circulated ice water around my injured knee, and she questioned the use of that but allowed me to keep it. She asked about the box that was on my bed. "Facial tissue," I said. While that question might seem overly simplified to the casual, non-geriatric observer, I knew that they frequently checked on the mental acumen of the patients by asking them easy questions like, "What's that box on your bed?" I proudly knew I had passed the rigorous inspection of the nursing supervisor, who, having completed her checklist, left.

The following day, I was eating my lunch in the common room when I spotted the nursing supervisor again. This time she was circling the dining tables, clipboard in hand, checking out everyone's eating habits. She seemed particularly concerned about the lady who needed the comfort of her baby doll to be able to eat. Suddenly, there was a flash of a pink baby bonnet, a wail of anguished torment, and the streak of the nursing supervisor racing down the hall, baby doll in hand. She had left the clipboard at the table as an apparent substitution for the baby doll, but it did nothing to improve the patient's appetite. My first thought was this must be some kind of "tough love" method of weaning people from baby dolls, and I let the incident pass. However, moments later, directly after a staff member had fluffed and arranged the throw pillows on the community couch, the nursing supervisor appeared again. She looked furtively around the room and, like an accomplished sneak thief, grabbed two of the fluffed throw pillows, stuffed them under her tunic, and raced down the hall. As a person who prided herself on figuring out who the murderer was long before the end of a movie and who had read every Nancy Drew mystery ever written, I quickly deduced that the nursing supervisor was **not** the nursing supervisor and that I ought to start monitoring who came into my room.

I chuckled at the antics of this older lady, and then, as I did at Walmart, I began to see myself in the women around me—women who needed baby dolls at meals and clipboards to make them feel important. Later that evening, the "nursing supervisor" appeared at my door, clipboard in hand, and told me she needed to confiscate my cup of ice. I gave her my ice, apologized for having it, and told her I wouldn't break the rules again. She made a notation on her clipboard and handed me a copy of her report. As she left with my ice cup, I looked down at the report and saw only a big heart drawn in the middle of the page. As I drifted to sleep that night, I thanked God that He had provided some comfort for these women and prayed that when I went to town with my clipboard, someone would lovingly hand me their cup of ice and ask if I'd like to hold their baby doll.

As my grandfather told my father, my father, at age ninety-nine, continues to tell me, "Don't ever get old, Jami; don't ever get old." Then we laugh and talk about our aches and pains, about what we had for lunch, and about who is driving us crazy politically. Every day I marvel at the grace with which my dad has aged. He had the selfless love that helped him decide to move with my mom to a retirement facility while they could still make that decision together. He gave up driving before it became too sore a subject, and he has now made the move to an assisted living apartment, realizing that he might need a little more daily help as he pushes for 100. I don't think my dad has ever had a clipboard or baby doll moment in his life, but he cared for my mom, who certainly did. Mother died of Alzheimer's just two months Max was killed, and maybe because Daddy and I shared a common time of grief, we now share a common understanding of the aging process. God has gifted with Daddy ninety-nine years of life thus far, and the beauty of that life has been that Daddy is ready and unafraid to go home to the Lord at whatever time the Lord decides.

Thinking about these ladies in my story, I am comforted to know that though their actions were less than rational, they were not unhappy. Having his world shrink to a tiny apartment and three trips to the dining room each day has not extinguished that twinkle in my dad's eye nor his innate kindness to those around him. These people are living simple satisfying lives.

Living through loss is often a moment in time that ages us emotionally. We may feel exhausted on a day when we do nothing but breathe. And we may be waiting for some special sign from God that all will be well. On the evening of my husband's accident, I opened my Bible to read through the Psalms because, as a Christian, I felt it was what I was supposed to do. I waited for God to bring immediate comfort for my pain. In my suffering, I cried out for God to show Himself. It didn't happen that night or the next, or the next. Oswald Chambers, in his book, *My Utmost for His Highest*, described my mind set perfectly: "We want to be conscious of God; we look for it in some cataclysmic event."[1]

As we age, we are blessed to be able to look back and see that God was there with us but without the need for a burning bush. However, in dealing with loss, it is sometimes hard to remember that truth; this is where our faith comes into the picture. Faith is our cornerstone, and the words of the Scriptures are the building blocks of that faith. God doesn't have to **show** himself to His children because He is *in* His children, directing our steps, our progress to a life filled with quiet moments when we know He is God.

Just before Max was killed, he had celebrated his sixty-seventh birthday and on the day of the accident, my granddaughter, Shirley Cate, (age five at the time and who, herself, had survived the accident in Max's truck), made a statement so wise beyond her years; it will resonate with me forever! She said, "Cappy had all the birthdays God wanted him to have." Knowing that God ordained the number of Max's birthdays plus yours and mine brings me comfort. God's unseen presence was there to take the Captain home.

I am living and getting older for all the years planned out by my Lord, as is my dad. People around me endure loss, pain, and disappointment in different ways. But resting in the assurance of a five-year-old's wisdom keeps me grounded, prepared to face what is ahead, and comforted that I am not the supervisor.

Reflections:

1. Do you fear aging? What are your specific fears?

2. Does getting older bring a sense of loss about things you have not gotten to do in your life? What are some of those things? Does the desire to do those things outweigh your desire for salvation?

3. Do you think accomplishments in life always depend on how long someone has lived? Give some examples where a short life brought great accomplishments.

4. Read Matthew 27:57–61. How old was Jesus when He died? How was He treated in death? Had He accomplished His goal?

5. How does God care for us after death? Read Revelation 21:4.

"Even unto your old age, I am he and to your gray hairs I will carry you. I have made and I will bear; I will carry and will save."

Isaiah 46:4

CHAPTER 13

"But Don't You Step on My Blue Suede Shoes"

Lyrics by Carl Perkins, performed by Elvis Presley

"All flesh is like grass and all its glory like the flower of grass. The grass withers and the flower falls, but the word of the Lord remains forever."

1 Peter 1:24–25

I'm sitting at the airport waiting to catch my flight to California to visit my dad. I just popped two ibuprofen tablets into my mouth because my knees hurt. Admittedly, these are old knees, but the aches and pains of today are due almost entirely to my recent fall.

I was in the middle of downtown Oxford, crossing the busiest street, arms full of a ridiculously large purse and all the pertinent papers needed for the meeting to which I was rushing. I had on my favorite pair of soft leather loafers that had been a wardrobe staple for at least ten years. They were a primary part of my shoe collection, but they no longer fit quite as well as they had ten years earlier. They flopped a bit in the heel and gave my toes a workout as I had to grip the inside lining to keep them from falling off.

Because I was slightly late for my lunch meeting, I was hurrying, but as is the norm for so many people in Oxford, I was attempting to look stunning while doing it. And though Oxford is the most socially elite town of the South (ask any Ole Miss Alum), the quality of street paving did not match the elite status.

One moment I was strolling briskly in my favorite stylish shoes in my favorite stylish town, looking every bit the stunning sixty-nine-year-old that I was when my toe caught a crack in the pavement and my stunning body sprawled face-down in the crosswalk at the height of the lunchtime rush hour.

Tires screeched and horns blew. Dying of embarrassment but wanting to maintain some semblance of a stunning persona, I quickly got up. A lady in the car closest to me leaned out of the window and yelled, "Are you okay?" I nodded in the affirmative and then proceeded to stumble to the pavement a second time.

By this time, no one was buying my attempt at nonchalance. The concerned lady got out of her car, as did a kind young man in the adjacent car. The woman picked up my disgorged purse, showing herself to be both compassionate and someone who knew the value of a fashionable handbag; the young man collected all my scattered papers, after which they both guided me to the curb. On the bright side, nothing was broken, and I immediately gave God a huge thank-you. On the downside, one shoe was still in the middle of the street.

The young man must have binge–watched Disney's *Cinderella* because he gallantly rushed to retrieve the shoe and then got down on one knee, á la Prince Charming, to place the blue loafer back onto my foot. It was a perfect fit.

As I shuffled down the street, more than a little mortified, I kept looking around to make sure no one I knew had seen my spectacular fall from grace. Just when I thought the coast was clear and the traffic began to move, a lady several cars back from the scene of the accident rolled down her window and yelled, "Love your cute shoes." Oxonians are acutely aware of stunning fashion statements.

When loss occurs, we often hang on to the familiar, finding comfort in the things we know and the way things used to be. Loss brings a new element to our lives, an element to which we are not accustomed; our lives don't seem to fit us anymore, just like my old shoes.

Might it have been vanity that had led me to keep those old shoes? They had been in vogue when I bought them, and I always felt I looked stylish in them—maybe not the Kardashians but definitely Doris Day. I continue to keep clothes long past their expiration dates because they are classics. I still have my cheerleading outfit from high school, though it hasn't fit for forty years. I finally gave up the pompoms when the cat mistook them for her litter box. And I have a closet full of clothes that are the result of impulse shopping; they appeared to make me look good while I was at the store but not when I got home. My hair looks perfect when the lady at the salon does it, but not when I do it. My makeup looks perfect when the lady at the makeup counter applies it, but the bags under my eyes miraculously reappear when I do my own makeup. Perhaps vanity wasn't what tripped me up but rather the desire for things to stay the same; with change often comes a sense of loss followed by the accompanying grief. We mourn for what "used to be."

Consider what happened when I was sprawled in the middle of the street. Someone stepped in to pick me up. Someone supported me when I fell. Someone made sure I was on my way again. But my *first* instinct was to look up from where I had fallen, to see if help was coming toward me, and that instinct was born out of the assurances offered by God: "Look to me and be gracious to me as is your way with those who love your name. Keep steady my steps according to your promise and let no iniquity get dominion over me" (Psalm 119:132-133).

Knowing that God measures each step I take reinforces that desire to "look up" for help, but all the help in the world will not allow our lives to stay the same. Each step is different, each thought is different, and each day dawns differently from the last, leading to a constantly changing set of circumstances that impact the way we live out our days.

Relationships change, jobs change, abilities change, and the social outlook of the country changes; we must all begin to wonder if there is any constant in our lives that will remain the same or be there when we look up for help as we fall. Christians can give a resounding "yes" to that question. The one constant that will remain the same is our savior, Jesus Christ, "the same yesterday, today and forever" (Hebrews 13:8).

My change from yesterday was the unexpected death of my husband. Max was a supremely good human being, touching so many lives in such positive ways. Still, he was a sinner, just like you and me. The changes in his life ended at age sixty-seven, at the bottom of a gully on the side of the road. But because Max was a believer in the gospel of Jesus Christ and His offered salvation as the constant in life, Christ was there at the bottom of that gully to pick Max up and take him to a place where change and loss could no longer hurt him. However, the living must continue to face the changes of today and the changes of the tomorrows yet to come.

Oswald Chambers' book, *My Utmost for His Highest*, again brings some wisdom to the discussion of difficult changes in our lives. He suggests that professed faith in Christ is important, but that faith is often bolstered up by feelings of blessedness, sanctification, and the assurance of redemption, in part because the believer has yet to suffer a great loss. However, he explains, to get to that place where you can be lifted back up when you suffer a great fall or a tremendous loss, faith must be tempered with the actualities of life: "When we once get there, no matter where God places us or what the inner desolations are, we can praise God that all is well. That faith is being worked out in actualities...Faith must be tested because it can turn into a personal possession only through conflict. Faith is unutterable trust in God, trust which never dreams that He will not stand by us."[1]

Christ faced the actualities of death on the Cross, but His faith that He was doing His father's will did not waver. His life lasted thirty-three short years, and yet that small window of time provided a goal to which we should all strive daily, forgetting changes that occurred in the past and not worrying about the changes to come in the future, to "find rest for your souls" (Jeremiah 6:16).

If you have suffered any kind of loss through the changes in your life, your faith is now being tested by actualities, just as Jesus was faced with the actualities of His life. And it is through His life you can see God's perfect plan in birth, in death, in lives well lived or in lives lost. We must strive to live each day accepting the grace and mercy provided to us by Christ's atoning blood on the Cross. When you look up, Christ will be the one to reach down and pick you up when you fall; He will be the one to heal your wounds, put your shoes back on your feet, and prepare you for another day. His steadfastness will allow you to live your life completely, each day to its fullest, all the while resting in His constancy and unchanging support. It is hoped that at the end of your life, like my granddaughter said about her "Cappy," you can say you had all the birthdays God wanted you to have and that a life well lived for Him is your testament to His unfailing love.

Reflections:

1. What has been the greatest change in your life?

2. Did you have help adjusting to that change? Read Psalm 91:9-12.

3. Are there moments in your life where you would like a "do-over"? Do you dwell on them or look ahead?

4. Have you helped to "lift" someone else up? How did it make you feel? How did they feel about your help? Read Isaiah 53:4a and Galatians 6:2.

"…we also believe, and so we speak, knowing that, he who raised the Lord Jesus will raise us also with Jesus and bring us with you into his presence. For it is all for your sake, so that as grace extends to more and more people it may increase thanksgiving and glory to God."

2 Corinthians 4:13a–15

CHAPTER 14

"A Horse Is a Horse, Of Course, Of Course"

Mister Ed theme song

"And he told them the parable to the effect that they ought always to pray and not lose heart."

Luke 18:1

Wally died and my son had to bury him.

This sounds so much more disturbing than it really was, and yet, coming so close on the heels of my husband's death, it did impact our family and taught us all another of God's truths.

Wally had been the chair of the School of Pharmacy at the University of Mississippi and a brilliant inventor, holding several patents on his formulas. He was also a great lover of the arts and culture. Together, he and his wife, Betty, served as the medical team for students traveling with the University of Mississippi, funded community beautification projects for the city of Oxford, and supported our church with both their singing voices and music purchases, not to mention Wally's leadership role as an church elder. But most important to me, Wally was a wonderful friend who loved the Lord and could kill a snake with a single shot from a .22 rifle at fifty yards.

When Wally died, Miss Betty carefully followed the instructions he had left for his memorial service. It included the selection of speakers and music. However, it was his request of having my son, Ryan, bury him that certainly got the attention of the Miller family.

Before Miss Betty's phone call regarding Wally's wishes, Ryan had not given much thought to burying a person. When we lost family pets, it was always Max or me who took care of kitty internment, wanting to spare our boys the trauma of that loss. The only thing Ryan had ever buried up to this point, other than his brother's Hot Wheel cars (in retaliation for Patrick's record player experiments) was a horse. And even then, the horse wasn't technically buried.

Family friend and horse owner, Miss Laura, called her able-bodied barn boy, Ryan, to tell him that Cuckleburr had died out in the pasture and that he would have to bury the horse *quickly* as it was July. By the time Ryan got to the pasture, Cuckleburr had been dead for a while and had become quite rigid; now I know why they call dead bodies "stiffs." Using the trusty John Deere with the frontloading attachment, Ryan scooped up Cuckleburr. With a horse head and torso in the scoop and four stiff horse legs out front leading the way, Ryan drove the tractor back to the house to ask about the final resting place for Cuckleburr.

Anyone who knew Miss Laura understood her to be a supremely practical person. There was to be no marker stating, "Cuckleburr, Beloved Horse and Friend" or "Here Lies Cuckleburr, Safe from the Glue Factory At Last" or even a chorus of "Home on the Range." Instead, Ryan was to drive the equine "stiff" down a hill beyond the riding ring, dig out part of the hillside, and insert Cuckleburr firmly into the indention.

Miss Laura handed Ryan a shovel, and he began to dig. After a few hours of digging, Ryan realized the compromised hillside into which

Cuckleburr was to be inserted would cause the collapse of the adjacent riding ring. Of perhaps greater importance was that Cuckleburr was too big and too stiff to fit into the hillside no matter how much Ryan dug it out. Miss Laura told Ryan to stuff the horse in as best he could and then cover him up with dirt, sticks and leaves, along with generous amounts from the nearby mound of manure.

It's easy to understand why, when Ryan received Miss Betty's request to bury Wally, his mind went immediately back to the tragic end of Cuckleburr.

Knowing that burying Wally required substantially more finesse than burying Cuckleburr, Ryan enlisted the help of his friend and colleague, Scott, instructing Scott to wear work clothes, work gloves, and to bring a shovel. Ryan added a posthole digger to the list of needed digging implements.

The two stalwart gravediggers arrived at Miss Betty's house to receive Wally's body, after which they would proceed to the old cemetery behind our beloved College Hill Church. Miss Betty held out a box. Both sudden understanding and relief shone brightly on Ryan's face. However, as he picked up the box, he noticed that it was held together with silver duct tape. Ryan cocked a questioning eyebrow, prompting Miss Betty to explain, "All of Wally wouldn't fit, and the box broke."

Not wanting to spill any more of Wally, Ryan and Scott painstakingly made their way back to the SUV and reverently placed the duct-taped package in the back seat. But before they could get on the road, Miss Betty came running from the house, waving a large screw-top jug of red wine, half empty. Her instructions were that once they got him into the ground, they were to pour the remaining wine over Wally—one of his last wishes and one of his favorite wines.

Off they drove to our church and the old cemetery beyond, with Ryan hoping they wouldn't get stopped by county law enforcement and have to explain why they had an open bottle of liquor, shovels, and a dead man in the back seat.

Ryan and Scott quickly got to work, digging a hole in front of the marker with Wally's name already inscribed on it and, in a dignified and reverent manner, they placed the duct-taped box into the finished space. They had just begun pouring the bottle of wine over the top of Wally when they heard a patient yet somewhat concerned voice. "What are you doing?"

It was our pastor, Justin, who was fairly new to our congregation and hadn't done many funerals. Ryan explained that they were burying Wally and pouring his favorite wine on top of him. To Justin's credit, he didn't flinch, recoil, or run. He just stared in wonder at the two guys in the graveyard with shovels and a hole filled with what appeared to be a roll of duct tape awash in red wine; at this point, one of the gravediggers asked, "Should we pray or something?" And the preacher did just that but not because he was speechless at finding a wine-soaked gravesite or because he didn't know what else to say.

Indeed, Justin understood that prayer is a means of communication with the Father, of connecting with God in a way so that we might better understand His plans, His ways, and His desire to treat us as His precious children. The preacher prayed for peace and solace for those grieving, thanksgiving for Wally's faithfulness and spoke aloud the promises of God in Christ. Prayers like those spoken at the graveside can put you in the very presence of God, and in that presence, the burden of loss is suddenly shared—*not removed* but shared.

In suffering through loss, we will most assuredly learn something critical about our relationship to God. Oswald Chambers explains: "We imagine we would be all right if a big crisis arose, but the crisis will only reveal the stuff we are made of; it will not put anything into you. Crisis always reveals character."[1]

Chambers continues to explain that "the private relationship of worshipping God is the great essential in fitness."[1] One component of that right relationship is prayer—daily prayer! Prayer does not protect us from a crisis; it makes us stronger, better equipped, and "fit" to deal with that event. Spending time in daily prayer to God opens our relationship to Him, where our sorrow can flow to Him and His strength to us. Even in the midst of a crisis, prayers of thanksgiving for who God is and for His love, mercy, offered grace and sacrifice will refocus our sorrow away from ourselves and back to the knowledge that the sovereign God loves us.

God appreciates our acknowledging His goodness in our prayers, but He doesn't need our prayers. *We need our prayers.* Our prayers keep us grounded in the knowledge that we are not the guiding force in our lives. Our focus must be firmly on God through prayer and meditation on the Scriptures, with a deep commitment to revere and glorify God. J.I.Packer, in his book, *Evangelism and the Sovereignty of God,* says, "The recognition of God's sovereignty is the basis for your prayers because you recognize that God is the author and source of all the good that you have had already and all the good you hope for in the future."[4]

When you suffer a loss, people often offer words of consolation. For me, they were statements like, "God needed Max more than you did," or "God needed another angel in heaven," or even the harsh truth, "It was God's will and you'll get over it." While I agree that loss is in the realm of God's plan for life, hearing things like this from people who could not feel my deep grief was hurtful. At these times of loss, you may not want to face anyone; people may seem to avoid you, not knowing what to say or how to say it. And your daily prayer time may give way to a sadness that is paralyzing in its depth.

I urge you to rest in that still small voice of God speaking to your heart, and be mindful of Psalm 46:10, where God inspired the Sons of Korah to write, "Be still and know that I am God." Remembering this scripture, remembering a God who loved me with such fervor, who had created my husband, and who went to the Cross for us both, helped me to understand that though people might not be able to relate to my grief and loss, God could because He had watched His loved one die as well. Through prayer, let God share your grief in a way no friend or family member ever could.

Praying to, talking with, and listening to the Father amplifies that still small voice. Praying puts us in the presence of the Father, supports us through the ministering of the Holy Spirit, and reminds us of Christ's sacrifice for our salvation.

Reflections:

1. Do you only pray at times of crisis or regularly? Do you have a special time or place you pray? Read 1 Thessalonians 5:17–18.

2. Are most of your prayers about your needs or prayers of thanksgiving, or are they an equal combination of both? Read 2 Corinthians 9:11, 15 and Philippians 1:9–11.

3. Do prayers have to be long? Can one sentence constitute a prayer?

4. How do you feel after praying?

"The LORD is near to all who call on Him, to all who call on Him in truth."

Psalm 145:18

CHAPTER 15

"A Book Report on Peter Rabbit"

Taken from *"You're a Good Man Charlie Brown"*
A musical by Clark Gesner

"I wait for the. LORD, my soul waits and in His word I hope."

Psalm 130:5

I play a game of Scrabble each morning before getting up, allegedly to keep my mind sharp and to grow my vocabulary should I ever want to write another book and in case I've used up all the really good words in this one. Playing Scrabble against the computer at the medium level has garnered me a 70% win rate; this isn't a monumental score, but I must admit to learning all the two-letter words that can be used to win a game on the last move.

Some of those words are fairly common and fit easily into my day-to-day conversations: "oh," as in "Oh my, I just beat the smugly confident computer again," or "hm," as in "hm, is that really a Scrabble word?" However, some of those two letter words make no sense outside of being used to win the game; they will never be used in my next book, should I write it: aa, ae, ai, qi, za, xu, and so on. There are 107 of these little gems.

According to Wikipedia, a word is "the basic element of language that carries an objective or practical meaning, can be used on its own, and is uninterruptible." We can speak, hear, sign, and write, and if you're a five-year-old—or just one at heart—you can even *eat* words with your alphabet breakfast cereal. In fact, some of us have frequently had to eat our words!

However, when we read words, our way of understanding that "basic element of language" becomes somewhat murkier. Take, for example the Charles Schulz characters of *Peanuts* as depicted in the Clark Gesner musical, *You're a Good Man, Charlie Brown.*[2] The *Peanuts* crew is asked to write a one-hundred-word book report on Beatrix Potter's *Peter Rabbit.* They've all read the same book, but depending on their mindsets and personal interests, their reactions are vastly different. Lucy approached her assignment as a nuisance that she considered beneath her. She rushed to finish with very little thought to the quality of the words she used or their content:

"Peter Rabbit is a stupid book about this stupid rabbit who steals vegetables from other peoples' gardens. 1,2,3,4,5,6,7,8,9,10,11,12,13,14,15,16,1 7! Hm, 83 more to go."

Charlie Brown just couldn't seem to get started. His mastery of the art of procrastination over the course of the three- day assignment left him without words and probably without the report:

"If I start writing now when I'm not really rested, it could upset my thinking which is no good at all. I'll get a fresh start tomorrow, and it's not due til Wednesday, so I'll have all of Tuesday unless something should happen."

Schroeder didn't want to think about the words on the pages of Beatrix Potter's book at all. His mind was elsewhere and he tried creatively to force Potter's words into his narrative of Robbin Hood:

"It reminded me of Robbin Hood...Just then an arrow flew in–Whing!

It was a sign for the fight to begin–Zing! And it looked like the sheriff would win–Ah! But not for long. Away they ran. Just like rabbits. Who run a lot. As you can tell from the story of Peter Rabbit which this book report is about."

And Linus took a simple children's book and turned it into an article to rival the thoughts of Judge Judy, Dr. Phil and Jerry Springer. The original words of *Peter Rabbit* were lost in his preconceived ideas that gave no thought to the author's intent:

"In this report I plan to discuss the sociological pressures so great as to drive an otherwise moral rabbit to perform acts of thievery which he consciously knew were against the law, not to mention the extreme pressure exerted on him by his deeply rooted rivalry with Flopsy, Mopsy and Cottontail." While it's clear that the characters from *Peanuts* were not at a loss for words regarding their assignment, we often are, especially when we encounter sorrow.

Loss that brings sorrow can leave us struggling for words; we cannot adequately express ourselves through language. Others in our lives may also feel that same inadequacy when they attempt to communicate with us in our grief.

But just as I learned in Scrabble, not all words are created equal. Through this book, I have sought to convey words of hope, understanding, comfort, insight, and shared experience. And though I might feel that all the words I have written came from my heart, they did not; they came from the Word of God, the Bible.

God inspired people to write His story. Their words are rich, truthful, and carefully chosen by God. His plot brings the pieces of lives together like a beautifully woven yet unfinished tapestry on which He works daily. In the Bible, the Lord has given us a great gift so that the stories of God's character, Christ's sacrifice and the indwelling of the Holy Spirit become the patterns for our daily living. His words are **timeless**: "My soul melts away for sorrow; strengthen me according to your word" (Psalm 119:28).

Reading the Bible is what inspires me to pray, to build a relationship with God. And studying the Bible is what led me to write these words in my book.

It's important to understand that the Bible is not just a series of individual books. While it is divided into two parts which are called the Old and New Testaments, these two Biblical parts are understood as historical markers of time. But *from beginning to end*, the entire Bible is the *complete* story of God's love for His creation and His plan for offered salvation through a savior; there is only *the testament* filling each and every page of the whole Bible. These pages can enlighten, support, comfort, and instruct you. The words of this book are truly "uninterruptible." They "will not pass away" (Matthew 24:35), they "abide in you" (John 15:7), they are "living and active" (Hebrews 4:12), and they "remain forever" (1Peter 1:25).

Unlike Lucy, don't stop at one hundred words, because in the Bible, each word is an inspired blessing, helping you to understand the hills and valleys of life: "How precious to me are your thoughts, O God! How vast is the sum of them! If I would count them, they are more than the sand" (Psalm 139:17–18a). Unlike Schroeder, let the stories, adventures, and lessons in the Bible fill your imagination and stir your soul; these stories are like no others because they are true: "He made my feet like the feet of a deer and set me secure on the heights. He trains my hands for war, so that my arms can bend a bow of bronze" (Psalm 18:33–34). Unlike Linus, though his interpretation was entertaining, don't let the sinful world intrude on the truths contained in the Bible; these truths are inspired and perfected by God: "Trust in the LORD with all your heart and do not lean on your own understanding" (Proverbs 3:5). And unlike Charlie Brown, don't put off opening the Bible, reading it, studying it and letting the words of God be your greatest means of healing sorrow and loss: "For the simple are killed by their turning away, and the complacency of fools destroys them; but whoever listens to me will dwell secure and will be at ease, without dread of disaster" (Proverbs 1:32–33).

Hear God's voice in His word, bringing you joy and calling you to life once again: "He put a new song in my mouth, a song of praise to our God" (Psalm 40:3).

Reflections:

1. When was the last time you opened and read the Bible?

2. Have you developed a reading plan for the entire Bible?

3. What parts of the Bible give you the most comfort? What parts of the Bible are the most difficult to read? What parts of the Bible are the most difficult to understand?

4. Do you think we should understand everything written in the Bible? Read Deuteronomy 29:29

5. Can you see the continuity between the Testaments of the Bible? Can you see the plan for the salvation offered by Christ throughout the entire Bible? Read Genesis 1:26, Hebrews 1:1–2 and Hebrews 2:10.

"Your word is a lamp unto my feet and a light unto my path."

Psalm 119: 105

EPILOGUE

"The LORD is near to the broken-hearted and saves the
crushed in spirit. Many are the afflictions of the righteous,
but the LORD delivers him out of them all."

Psalm 34:18-19

When I began writing this book, it was originally a series of letters in a journal written to my husband, telling him what had happened in my life and the lives of our family members since he had died. The original working title was *Dear Captain Max: Joy Comes with the Mourning.*

After working on it for almost two years, I adjusted the text to be more inclusive for everyone; I recognized that loss and the accompanying grief comes in many forms, not just because of the death of a loved one. The stories remained the same, but I hoped that readers would understand that I was now writing these "letters" to them.

Since starting my adventure in Christian writing, I have, of course, suffered a few more difficulties in my life and have been continually rereading all that I had written in this book to keep myself grounded in the Lord.

My son, who was my next-door neighbor and slayer of snakes, informed me that he had been offered a new and exciting job, which entailed a move to the state capitol, Jackson, Mississippi. He suggested that I think about whether or not to stay in our small little town of Oxford or move to Jackson.

Naturally, I shed many tears and spent numerous sleepless nights trying to decide what to do. Each night I would give the problem over to the Lord, and each morning I would take it back again. And I reread this book. After a lot of praying, gnashing of teeth, and panic attacks, but with the peace of Christ in my heart, I made my decision to move. I told my friends of my decision and began praying for an easy transfer from the old homestead and for a new and *affordable* place to live, preferably within close proximity to the Grands.

My house sold on the first day it went on the market and for the full asking price. The gentleman who managed my small investments called that same day to say he had discovered a way for me to make a larger down payment on a new house. I quickly found a house I could afford—the smallest house on the smallest lot in a very nice neighborhood. The sellers readily accepted my offer. I found a transfer company I could afford, and I managed all the many insane details that go along with a big move. It only took me two full months to unpack every box and find a place for almost everything.

I close with this story of my escapades to let you know that though this was my twentieth move, it was my first without my husband at my side. With the details involved in buying and selling a house as well as the physical move resting squarely on only my shoulders, I forged ahead and now have number twenty under my belt. Lately, I have heard myself proudly say, "I did it all by myself."

But nothing could be further from the truth. God, as He promised, lifted that massive burden from my shoulders and smoothed that bumpy, unknown road I was headed down. My friends and church prayed for me daily, and I felt supported by those prayers. All the pieces of the puzzle that God was working on in my life interlocked, fitting together perfectly because *He*, not I, supervised the move.

However, this move was an onslaught against the wall of security I had begun to rebuild around myself after my husband's death. My new wall began to crumble, even before the mortar was set. The move represented other *big losses*: a home of twenty-two years; living next door to my family; the familiarity of and love for my church family; the friendships of the man at the hardware store, the girl at the pharmacy, the antique store owner, the barber who cut my hair, my doctors, the auto mechanic, the wonderful mail lady, and the waitress at the Beacon restaurant, plus the collective memory of my community about Captain Max, and so much more.

Joyfully, I want you to know what I found in my new town: a house that's just right for me and the cat plus the new kitten I acquired along the way, a place for my piano, the Grands living only seven minutes away, a new church and a new church choir, along with the ever-present sense that God was with me in every facet of this move. After two months here, I know where the screwdrivers are. After two months here, I know where the potholes are in the roads that I travel. After two months I know the lady at the fabric store by name and that my new neighbor likes cats.

These are not big accomplishments, but God doesn't require "big" from me. He just requires that I rest daily in His loving care, trusting Him to put things into place as He would have them. And when I shed tears over the things I lost in my former life, I continue to listen for that still small voice that tells me that together, God and I can achieve joy and peace, and that no loss is too great for the Lord.

A friend texted me the other day and asked if I was happy. I responded that I was "content" and that "happy" would come. I'll accept contentment for now because I know God, as He promised, is working on "happy." And that happiness will turn my "joy in the mourning" into "joy in the morning" as I face each new dawn with God as my loving father, with Jesus Christ as my Messiah, giving all He had to redeem my soul, and with the Holy Spirit walking ahead of me, behind me, beside me, and within me.

"Weeping may tarry for the night, but joy comes in the morning . . . .
You have turned my mourning into dancing."
Psalm 30:4, 11

NOTES

1. Oswald Chambers, *My Utmost for His Highest*: (London, England: Dodd, Mead and Company, 1935).

2. Gesner, Clark, *You're a Good Man Charlie Brown*: (Robbinsdale, MN: Fawcett Press, 1967).

3. C.S. Lewis, *Mere Christianity*: (New York, NY: Harper One, 2001).

4. J. I. Packer, *Evangelism and the Sovereignty of God:* (London, England:InterVarsity Press, 1961).

5. Ray C. Stedman, *Talking with My Father: Jesus Teaches on Prayer* (Grand Rapids. MI: Discovery House Publishing, 1997).

6. James Strong, *The New Strong's Expanded Exhaustive Concordance of the Bible* (Nashville, TN: Thomas Nelson, 2001).